T•O•U•C•H•I•N•G

Cloudbase

The Complete Guide to Paragliding
3rd Edition

by
Ian Currer and Rob Cruickshank

First and second editions published by Leading Edge Press & Publishing Ltd
ISBN 0-948135-27-1; ISBN 0 948135-41-7

Third, revised and updated edition by Air Supplies, March 1996

© Ian Currer/Robin Cruickshank/Leading Edge Press & Publishing, 1991, 1992
© Air Supplies/Robin Cruickshank 1996

A CIP Catalogue record for this book is available from the British Library.

ISBN 0 9528862 0 0

Text by Ian Currer
Illustrations by Robin Cruickshank
Edited by Stan Abbott
Page design by Barbara Allen
Cartoons by Bill Lehan
Design and type by Leading Edge Press & Publishing Ltd ©
Colour reprographics by Impression, Leeds
Printed and bound in Great Britain by Ebenezer Baylis and Son Ltd, Worcester

Front cover: *It's a tough life! One of the Apco Aviation test pilots hard at work soaring the Mediterranean sea breezes. Glider: Apco Xtra*

• FOREWORD •

by Bernard Kane MBE
Former Chairman of the British Association of Paragliding Clubs' Safety and Training Committee

In a sport that is rapidly expanding and constantly developing there is a great need for suitable literature. This book by Ian Currer and Robin Cruickshank is a valuable addition to the existing, if somewhat meagre, number of publications on self-launch paragliding.

Ian, already a senior instructor with the British Hang Gliding Association, was one of the first to recognise the potential of the accelerating performance of paragliding canopies and he set out to master this new aspect of flying. The way in which he undertook to acquire these new skills and knowledge was typically well-organised and responsible. He asked for advice, attended a course of instruction and then attached himself to a training club. Given his existing flying and instructional skills his progress was smooth and fairly fast and it was not long before he took a BAPC instructor examination at which he was noted as the outstanding candidate of the year. He went on to run an excellent training establishment at which he made important contributions in the developing techniques of training paraglider pilots. In due course he became a BHPA Examiner and has become a member of the BHPA Safety and Training Committee. In 1994 Ian was appointed co-ordinator of the BHPA Training and Coaching panel.

This book takes a different approach to other publications on paragliding and, in my opinion, it benefits greatly accordingly. It is based upon a course or a series of courses taking a newcomer to the sport through the initial stages of training right through to advanced flying. It is not a 'do it yourself' manual but is a valuable reinforcement, an excellent guide and a treasure of information and advice on all matters appertaining to flying paragliders.

To the novice pilot it is a text book that lays out clearly each stage of the programme of training that he has undergone and is a reminder of what he was taught and what he is expected to know. It will be a great help towards achieving the Student and Club Pilot ratings. However, it would be quite wrong to look upon this book as suitable only for the novice, the person striving for the Pilot or Advanced Pilot ratings will find it equally useful as it covers the whole spectrum of advanced flying. I commend this book to you.

Bernard Kane

• CONTENTS •

• INTRODUCTION •

If you choose or have chosen a course in paragliding, you will quite soon find that your dreams of walking on air and soaring like a bird are beginning to be realised.

There are many challenges, and it will take some time and effort to become a competent pilot, but it will be worth it for the rare experience of being one of the few who can enjoy truly free flight.

This handbook is meant as an aid to learning, and can be referred to throughout, and after, your course.

IT IS NOT A TEACH-YOURSELF MANUAL.

Paragliding is perhaps the simplest and easiest form of aviation, thousands of people from all walks of life and a variety of age groups enjoy its unique appeal. But, like all adventure sports, paragliding can result in injury or death through error or ignorance, or if practised in the wrong conditions.

THE ONLY SAFE WAY TO LEARN IS TO BE TRAINED BY A PROFESSIONAL QUALIFIED INSTRUCTOR.

If you have any questions on any topic in this handbook or anything to do with flying do not hesitate to ask your instructor — there is no substitute for experience, and he or she will be glad to help.

Throughout this book, both pilots and instructors are referred to as "he". This is only for the sake of writing style: paragliding is in many ways an ideal sport for women, and is certainly one in which women can participate on equal terms.

A video and a CD ROM of *Touching Cloudbase* are also available. In them many of the techniques, subjects and equipment referred to in this book are illustrated. Copies should be available from wherever you bought this book. Alternatively you can order them from:

Ian Currer, Dunvegan Lodge, York YO4 5RY. Tel: 44 (0) 1759 304404 Fax: 44 (0) 1759 306747.

• GETTING STARTED •

A brief history

Back in the 1940s — on the east coast of America, just down the road from the site of the Wright brothers' first successful flights — another aviation pioneer was conducting experiments with kites made of pieces of curtain material. His name was Dr Francis Rogallo and, after much persuasion, his work was eventually followed up by his employers, the North American Space Administration. It was 1948 when he filed for a patent for his flexible Delta kite. From Dr Rogallo's work came a whole mountain of research, testing, and flexible wing (flex-wing) construction technology.

This resulted in both the Ryan Aircraft Company's bizarre looking aerial cargo-delivery wings — which used a folding "kite" wing — and the steerable recovery parachutes used by the Gemini series in the US space programme. But by far the most important offshoot of this research, as far as we are concerned, is that the Rogallo wing was utilised by several latterday aviation pioneers as an excellent way of getting off the ground, either by means of a tow-launch behind a boat or a car, or by foot-launching. Some of the earliest exponents of "hang gliding" (so-called because, in those days, you literally had to hang on by your armpits) made their wings from bamboo, polythene and sticky tape. Not surprisingly, the golden rule was never to fly higher than you care to fall.

Very soon, the machines were being made of stronger stuff and, as early as 1961, Tom Purcell Junior was tow-launched on a Rogallo wing in the USA. The following year, John Dickenson, a water-skier, began to fly a Rogallo wing in preference to the flat kites that had sometimes been used. It was he who introduced the idea to two men whose names are recognised by hang glider pilots worldwide today — Bill Moyes and Bill Bennett. These two dominated the early

Right: A standard hang glider in 1974. Note the seated pilot position, and lack of any battens in the sail. These craft achieved glide ratios of about 4:1

7

development of the sport of hang gliding as we know it today, and are still active as manufacturers in Australia and the USA respectively.

Meanwhile, in the UK, Walter Neumark was flying new types of parachute, designed by Lemoigne and Pioneer, which were capable of far superior performance and control than the existing types. Even back in 1961 Neumark, a sailplane pilot, could envisage a self-inflating parachute being used for soaring flight. Shortly afterwards, he wrote a manual, *Operational procedures for ascending parachutes*, and training began in what was to become known as parascending.

In 1968 Dan Poynter recorded in an article for *Parachutist* magazine that canopies were foot-launched at Lake Placid, in the USA, during the annual parachute competition. In 1973 the British Parachute Association withdrew support for the emerging sport of parascending and the British Association of Parascending Clubs was formed. In 1989, the association changed its name to the British Association of Paragliding Clubs, reflecting its interest in a range of related pursuits, from over-water towing operations, towed parascending and, most recently, foot-launched paragliding.

It was not until about 1980 that parachutes were foot-launched regularly from hills. At first it was a small minority of pilots, mostly in the French and Swiss Alps who began to emulate the hang glider pilots by launching from the steep slopes with their ram-air "rigs", but the sport was to grow with surprising speed. In the UK there was Gerald Williams, a lone hang glider pilot who could be seen drifting to earth beneath his canopy in the Peak District while his fellows shook their heads and muttered that it would never catch on. In the intervening years the sport of hang gliding itself had become firmly established: the brightly coloured wings were to be seen on mountainsides on every continent but Antarctica. Agreements were made with landowners for the use of their hills, training procedures were established and a great deal was learnt about the performance and stability of these extraordinary aircraft. Cross-country flights of hundreds of miles were made; even club pilots regularly used thermal and wave lift to gain thousands of feet of altitude. As the performance of the craft improved, so too did the expense and the time required to learn to fly them. Despite the lure of being able to soar like a bird the sport has always been for the few who had the considerable determination to carry the 70lb craft up the hill time and time again during their training, and the courage to attempt what can appear a frightening or dangerous activity (although, of course, with current equipment and training techniques, hang gliding is in reality nowhere near as dangerous as many people imagine).

In the early 1980s everything was in place for the birth of foot-launched paragliding as we know it today — the expertise and example of the hang gliding fraternity and the high performance ram-air canopies. The canopies being used were initially jump chutes designed to withstand the stresses of opening in free-fall. It very soon became apparent that these stresses were not present with the less abrupt inflation of a self-launch, and very soon manufacturers sprang up producing wings made of non-porous material. Such fabrics would probably cause a modern paraglider to explode if it was opened by a free-falling sky-diver at terminal velocity, but it offered a major performance advantage. Jump chutes also had to inflate evenly and rapidly and — as competitions often involve a near vertical descent to achieve target accuracy — these design criteria had led to the evolution of square canopies with very large cell entries and docile behaviour in the stall.

The paragliding manufacturers, however, had different criteria. They were looking for a very slow rate of descent and a good gliding performance and — as the wing was inflated before launch — they could afford to be less particular

Rigging and checking a hang glider takes about 20 minutes

about instant opening. Very soon paragliders diverged totally from their jump chute roots: they utilised high-lift aerofoils, narrow cell entries and long slender wings, more akin to the shape of a hang glider.

In terms of aircraft development, the evolution of the hang glider had been remarkable. There had been precious little research done on the behaviour of aerofoils at speeds below 40mph but, even so, every year the designers and manufacturers came up with significant improvements in performance and stability.

There had, of course, been a number of failures, some of them fatal, and the national associations of the major hang gliding nations had introduced test-bed facilities so that each new design could be thoroughly checked before being given a certificate of airworthiness. If the development of hang gliders had been remarkable, that of paragliders was (and is) positively meteoric, with new and improved designs appearing on an almost monthly basis, though there are signs now of a slow-down, mirroring the hang glider's development curve of the 70s & 80s.

Fortunately, because the national association in most countries is the same for both sports, the idea and the equipment for testing was already in place and in virtually all European countries at least, there is a mandatory test programme for new designs. At the time of writing the distance record for a paraglider is 330 kilometres, achieved by circling and climbing in thermals and hopping from one cloud to the next in the same way as hang gliders and sailplanes have been doing for years. But perhaps more significant than this is the sheer number of people who are attracted to the sport; in Alpine countries they number tens of thousands, and the activity

9

is growing very rapidly in places as diverse as the UK, Australia, North and South America, India, and the Far East. In the UK the sport has been (unusually) administered solely by the British Association of Parascending (later Paragliding) Clubs. In December 1990 the association voted to allow negotiations to begin to amalgamate with the British Hang-Gliding Association into on body. The following year — after much debate — the BHGA passed a similar motion. In 1992 the two associations amalgamated to form the British Hang-gliding and Paragliding Association.(BHPA).

❷ Introducing the equipment

The canopy

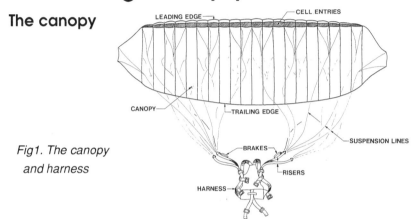

Fig1. The canopy
and harness

A paraglider is a simple aircraft, but in common with all other aircraft it is in fact the result of complex and painstaking design. Small changes in line lengths or subtle alteration of the cut of the fabric can make the difference between a sweet responsive wing or one with poor characteristics. The canopy is constructed of a top and bottom surface joined by a number of vertical segments. The resulting chambers are called cells. They have an opening at the front — the leading edge. These cell entries are covered with mesh on some models. Large entries generally indicate a slower and more stable aircraft; narrow or valved entries are found on craft on which the aim is to maximise performance. Each cell is separated from its neighbours by an inter-cell wall. These define the shape of the wing section: the more inter-cell walls, the more uniform the shape. These walls feature several holes, or ports, so that the air can pass from one cell to the next, helping to keep the internal pressure balanced and the wing evenly inflated. When it is fully inflated, the cell takes up an aerofoil shape with a flattish lower surface and a curved, or cambered, top surface. The point of maximum thickness usually occurs between 15 and 30 per cent of the way back from the leading edge.

The rear of the wing is called the trailing edge. On a typical canopy there may be anything from 30 to 100 cells. Often those in the centre will be longer than those at the tips, giving the canopy a tapered or elliptical shape; this shape,

when viewed from above, is called the planform. Some canopies may have
vertical areas at the tips, known as stabilos or "ears". Their function is to provide
stability, stretch the wing as they are forced outwards, and reduce induced drag.
Whether or not they actually achieve this reduction in drag is open to debate:
they certainly provide a handy place for the manufacturers to put their names!

A paraglider canopy is an inflatable wing; it is no longer correct to think of
it as a parachute. Most wings used for foot-launching will not "parachute" in the
true sense of the word except in very limited circumstances. They are either
gliding, if the wing has a suitable airflow over it, or stalled. In the latter case they
will probably collapse as internal pressure is lost. One of the major factors that
distinguishes a paraglider from a parachute is the material from which it is
made. Paragliders use non-porous fabrics (either nylon or polyester) which give
much better performance than those used in free-fall canopies. Fluorescent
colours are often used, although it is worth knowing that the chemicals that give
the "glow" to these colours do shorten the life of the fabric. Occasionally the
wing may feature battens made of plastic or glass fibre. These are sewn into the
sail to help retain the shape. "Flares" of heavier material, such as Mylar, do the
same job and help to distribute the load from the lines over a larger area.

The lines

The lines are made of very strong materials so that they can be kept thin so
as to minimise drag and weight. There are two main types: Kevlar, which is a
polyaramid (carbon fibre) material and is usually encased in an outer sheath of
Dacron (terylene) or something similar, and polyethylene, usually known as
Dyneema or Technora (Spectra in the USA). Polyaramid material is extremely
strong and has excellent resistance to stretching, or shrinking. It is not temperature sensitive. However it requires regular checking as it can easily be damaged
by kinking or knotting around a small radius.

Polyethylene is also very strong and it is more flexible too which tends to
prolong its life especially with hard use. However it is more likely to stretch or
shrink and is fairly temperature sensitive so lines of this material should be
protected from high temperatures (being left in a car in full sun for example). The
golden rule with all line material is to check it regularly both for stretch, shrink-
age and strength.

For more details on the properties of line materials see section 21: care of
your canopy.

In order to minimise drag and make the whole construction less complex,
the lines branch into two (or more) about half way up their length. Lines are
referred to by their position on the canopy, A-lines being those at the leading
edge, and C or D-lines being those at the rear. The control lines which are
attached to the trailing edge and terminate in a handle on the rear riser are often
produced in a distinctive colour to make them easy to locate.

The risers

The risers (known as V-lines in some countries) connect the canopy lines to the harness. Usually made of one-inch, or 25mm, webbing, they transfer the loads from the harness through the lines. There is usually one attachment point on each side of the harness to which the bottom of the risers are connected with a maillion or carabiner. The tops of the risers (of which there may be three or four per side) terminate in small steel maillons or links to which the lines are attached. The risers give the pilot a convenient single point to hold when launching and make it simple to swap one harness for another without disconnecting lines. The rear risers also feature small rings, or keepers through which the control lines pass. These, as the name suggests, prevent the control lines flying away out of reach in the wind. The control handles themselves, attached to these lines, are usually fastened to the riser by some easy-release system such as Velcro or a popper. Virtually all modern canopies have an accelerator system attached, operated by a foot stirrup. A few may feature weight shift bars or hand operated accelerators or trimmer systems. *These are mentioned again on page 100.* There have also been a few designs that included a harness as an integral part of the canopy.

The harness

Paragliding harnesses follow the same basic pattern — a wooden or plastic seat, a fabric back with webbing leg-loops and shoulder straps. In front of the body there is either a single waist strap or an arrangement of diagonally crossed straps. The latter type prevent the pilot from assisting turns made with the controls by moving his weight across to one side, but they do make the canopy more stable in some situations. Most recent models offer the facility to have either arrangement, and may include other features, such as attachments for accelerator systems, back protection devices or rear-mounted reserve compartments. All harnesses are adjustable so you can vary the size, shape and flying position. There are a great variety of harnesses to choose from and these are covered in greater detail on page 55.

③ # How a paraglider flies

When a paraglider is fully inflated it forms a solid wing which creates lift in the same way as that of a conventional aircraft. In order to fly it must create enough lift to carry its own weight and that of its pilot, and it achieves this with gliding flight. The wing is constantly flying forwards and downwards through the air and in doing so provides a flow over the aerofoil section. At first glance, a paraglider only has part of an aerofoil — the front bit appears to be missing

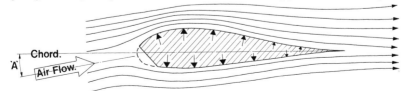

Fig 2. Airflow around a wing section. 'A' = angle of attack

where the cell entries are but, in fact, the build-up of pressure inside the canopy does back up and form a kind of false leading edge of air. *See fig 2.*

So how does an aerofoil work? Look at fig 2. The molecules of air that hit the leading edge are divided into two streams — those over and those under the canopy. Those below it are striking the lower surface at a shallow angle and creating a high pressure area. About one third of the aerofoil's lift is derived from this "push". The molecules that pass over the top surface, however, are obliged to follow a longer path as they are forced upwards over the cambered top surface. As the curve continues, the flow is deflected further upwards, while at the same time the air above the aerofoil is doing its level best to carry on in the same direction without altering course. This process is strengthened by the natural tendency of the air to drift away from the curved surface — rather like a car going round a bend at speed. The result of this is that the air flowing over the top of the section is squeezed between the physical barrier of the wing below it and the inertia of the "normal" air above it.

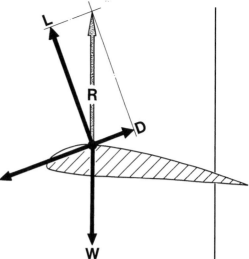

Fig 3. Forces on a wing. L = lift; D = drag; W = weight; V = forward velocity along flight path; R = resultant lifting force opposing weight.

It behaves exactly like water being squeezed through a narrow space (like the end of a hose-pipe) by accelerating, so the air is travelling more quickly over the top surface. At this point the physics become a little more complex but the result of this acceleration is that the pressure reduces (Bernoulli's theorem). This low pressure area generates a pulling force and contributes about two thirds of the lifting force of the wing.

So far we have established two forces acting on the canopy — gravity, which is acting to pull us down, and lift, acting upwards and slightly forwards. There is a third force as well — drag. This acts opposite to our direction of travel and reduces the speed and efficiency on the wing. The lift and drag combined are shown in fig 3 as R — the resultant. *(Drag is mentioned in more detail in Chapter 5, Terms).* When all these forces are in equilibrium, the wing will glide at a specific rate. This glide path is the Result. (V) — *see Fig 3.* Providing the canopy is flying with sufficient speed and at a suitable angle of attack, it will continue to glide correctly. What happens if we disturb this equilibrium?

Firstly, let us suppose that the angle of attack is too low. This is not readily achievable in normal flight as, at high speeds, the drag created becomes too great to permit any further acceleration. However, if too low an angle is achieved, the soft aerofoil begins to deform and, as the cell entries can not work, the wing will collapse at the front. This is known as a "tuck" and is quite easy to bring about if the pilot is stationary on the ground. In the air the pilot tends automatically to swing under the canopy to the correct position but a tuck can happen in flight if the pilot has induced a low angle of attack in recovering from a stall for example, or in turbulent air. A paraglider is generally fixed in its angle relative to the pilot (unless trim devices are fitted), but we can alter the angle of attack by use of the controls. There is a ratio between the lift and drag generated, and by adding more drag (by braking) we can alter that ratio. This means that the wing is now moving forwards less rapidly and the airflow is at a higher angle of attack. If you look up as you add brake you can see the leading edge of the canopy move back slightly as it takes up a more rearward position. The initial result of this is an increase in the amount of lift — the greater the pressure difference between the top and bottom surfaces, the greater the lift. The point of maximum lift is known as the minimum sink-rate. However, if the angle is increased too much, the air is unable to flow smoothly over the curve and the point at which the airflow breaks away (which in normal flight is next to the trailing edge) rushes forwards across the aerofoil until almost all the top surface is covered in a turbulent flow. The low pressure area is broken up and the wing ceases to work. This situation is a stall — *see fig 4.*

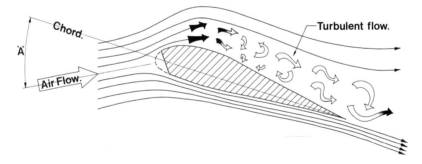

Fig 4. A stalled wing section caused by too high an angle of attack (A)

Some canopies in certain circumstances will find a point of equilibrium even with an angle of attack that is too high. The wing remains inflated but, because it has little or no forward speed, it is unable to generate sufficient lift and sinks very rapidly. This state is known as a "deep" or "parachutal" stall. *(See fig 5)* If forward motion is lost altogether, by a sharp application of maximum brake for example, the internal pressure will drop and the cells will deflate. The aerofoil section is then lost. This is a "dynamic" or "full" stall. Both deep and dynamic stalls can be recovered from easily though this may involve considerable altitude loss — *see Chapter 29. Stall recovery.* For this reason, a paraglider — like all aircraft — should be flown at slightly above the absolute minimum speed to ensure a margin for error.

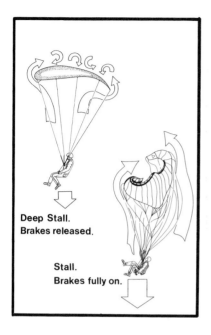

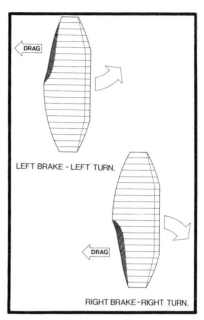

Fig 5   *Fig 6*

The controls and how they work   ❹

   Some paragliders can be steered by "weight-shift" and most models have accelerator stirrups to add extra speed, but all of them rely principally upon the control lines. The term "controls" is used rather than the common name of brakes because, in addition to their function in controlling speed, they are also used for steering and to stabilise the canopy in the event of a collapse. Each control is a single line, usually colour-coded to prevent confusion with the suspension lines. Unlike them, it is not attached to the riser directly but runs through a ring or "keeper" attached to the rear riser, and ends in a handle. The top of the control line is divided to attach to the trailing edge at several points.

   When the pilot pulls down one of the controls, the trailing edge of the canopy on that side is deflected downwards into the airflow. *(Fig 6)* This has two effects — the first is to increase the angle of attack of that side of the canopy slightly and increase the lift generated. The second effect is massively to increase the drag and reduce the airspeed of that side. These two effects work against each other, one trying to turn the canopy one way and one the other. On most conventional aircraft this creates the problem known as adverse yaw, which is usually overcome with the addition of a rudder. But on a canopy, the drag created in this way is far more effective than any opposing effect of lift and the craft will always turn towards the deflected side. If both controls are depressed at the same time, the wing will slow down uniformly and will also create slightly more lift. The further the controls are depressed the more drag is created and the slower the wing will fly until, eventually, the canopy will have such a high angle of attack that the wing will stall.

Obviously, if the canopy is being flown slowly and one control is raised this will also produce a turn. The steepest turns are achieved by simultaneously raising one side and depressing the other. **CAUTION** — it is possible to stall one half of the wing in this way and enter a spin. The controls also have three other uses: the first is on the ground during a reverse launch where they can be used to change the height and position of the "wall". The second is to collapse the canopy after landing or if you are being dragged — see *Touchdown and canopy control in Chapter 17*. The third use is to aid recovery from various unstable situations — tucks etc — *see Chapter 29, Canopy instability exercises*.

The controls are the equivalent of brakes and steering wheel on a car. It is vital that they are in good order and free of hitches or wear. They are also the easiest part of the canopy to get into a tangle — always use the Velcro or poppers provided to attach the controls to the riser after every landing.

⑤ Terms

Centre of pressure

Different areas of the aerofoil and the span of the canopy produce varying amounts of lift. For the purposes of showing this force, the term "centre of pressure" is often used. Literally this is the centre of pressure difference, a theoretical balance point through which the lift can be said to act.

Drag

This term has already been mentioned a number of times. What is drag? This is the thing that holds us back! It is the resistance of the air to anything passing through it, and it can be divided into two categories.

Parasitic drag — Friction caused by any surface or obstruction (pilot, lines etc). The faster you travel through the air the more parasitic drag you create. Doubling your speed quadruples the drag. Parasitic drag can be subdivided again into components such as skin friction and profile drag (the latter relates to the turbulence caused, for example, by moving a non-lifting surface through the air).

Induced drag — The action of an aerofoil disturbs the air as it passes through and this creates induced drag. There is always a little drag induced at the trailing edge where the airflow from above and below the aerofoil meet again at slightly different speeds. The majority of the induced drag, however, is created at the wingtips. The area of lower pressure above the wing is "attractive" to the air at a higher pressure below the wing. But, at the wing-tips, it is easier for the air to flow around the end of the wing and this is what happens. The result is a vortex at each tip — *see fig 7.*

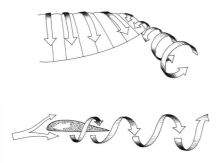

Fig 7. Pressure at tips. Wing tip vortices: At the tips, the pressure difference between the upper and lower surfaces is equalised by the air flowing up around the end of the wing. As the canopy moves forward it leaves a trail of rotating air behind each tip. This is the prime cause of induced drag. (And the cause of 'wake turbulence' often encountered downwind of an aircraft.)

Some designs feature "stabilos" or "ears" at the tips and one of their intended functions is to try and minimise this problem. The high aspect-ratio (long thin) wings that are becoming more common reduce this problem in the same way as hang gliders, sailplanes and albatrosses — simply by having a relatively smaller area of wing-tip. Induced drag reduces with speed, so there is a certain point at which parasitic and induced drag combine to give an optimum total figure. This is the speed at which the "glide ratio" is best.

L/D Ratio (glide angle)

L= lift and D = total drag, so the best L/D ratio occurs when the lift is greatest relative to the drag. *See fig. 8.* In practice this means when the canopy is flown at the speed where it will cover the most distance from a given height. For example, if a paraglider has an L/D of 6:1, it will glide 600 metres along for every 100 metres of altitude lost. This figure can only really be used as a comparative guide to the performance of the canopy. When you are actually in the air, any wind

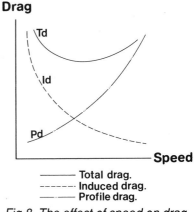

Drag

——— Total drag.
------- Induced drag.
—·—·— Profile drag.

Fig 8. The effect of speed on drag

or any lifting or sinking air will distort the performance by several hundred percent in either direction.

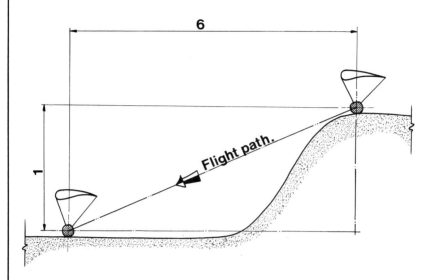

Fig 9. 6: 1 Glide ratio

Sink rate

If you read manufacturers' information sheets another figure you may see quoted is minimum sink rate. This refers to the slowest rate at which the canopy will descend through the air. If your minimum sink rate is, say, 1.5 metres per second, then the canopy will always be descending through the air at at least that rate. To soar, of course, the trick is to find some air rising faster than you are sinking. The minimum sink rate is usually found at the lower end of the canopy's speed range.

Aspect ratio

The aspect ratio is a measure of the canopy's shape. When a paraglider is laid out flat, the planform (shape viewed from above) can give us clues about the characteristics and likely performance of the wing. A high number probably means high performance and lower stability, though of course all manufacturers are struggling to improve the first without compromising the second. An albatross or a sailplane will have a very high aspect ratio whereas a paraglider or a songbird will have a low one.

Aspect ratio is calculated by dividing the square of the span by the area. For example a canopy with a span of 10.5 metres and an area of 25 square metres would work out as 10.5 x 10.5 = 110.25 divided by 25 = an aspect ratio of 4.41. This is a relatively slim wing and likely to have good performance.

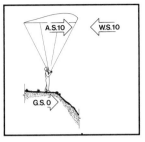

A

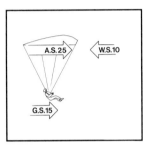

B

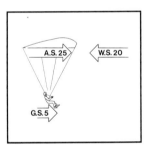

C

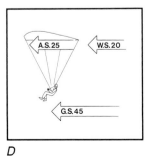

D

Windspeed, groundspeed and airspeed

Windspeed is simply the speed of the wind over the ground. Groundspeed is the speed of the aircraft relative to the ground. Airspeed is the speed of the airflow over the aerofoil. A point worth noting is that, in flight, some pilots have trouble distinguishing between airspeed and groundspeed. Take a look at the illustration.

A. The pilot is standing on top of a hill with an inflated canopy. The windspeed is 10mph, the ground-speed is 0mph and his airspeed is 10mph.

B. Now he has taken off. The windspeed is still 10 mph and his groundspeed is now 15mph. As he is flying into wind, the airspeed over the canopy must be 25mph. So far so good.

C. Now our pilot has encountered a 20 mph windspeed, his airspeed is still 25 mph. His ground-speed has dropped to 5 mph.

D. As he is a long way from the hill, he decides to turn around and fly back. He does not alter his airspeed which remains 25 mph and the windspeed is still 20mph. His flight path is now downwind and his groundspeed is now 45mph. Bear in mind that the 180° turn only took one second or so to complete, yet in that time groundspeed rose from 5mph to 45mph. The sudden increase in speed over the ground can be disconcerting if the pilot is not prepared and particu-larly as he may now be heading straight towards the hill. Pilots have been known to slow down at this point by braking hard, the result is, of course, a stall which can mean losing control and hitting the hill with painful consequences. It is easy to avoid this mistake by

— knowing what to expect

— judging your airspeed not by the ground, but by the feel of the airflow in your face and the position of the controls. If the wind is not blowing directly onto the hill the same thing occurs to a lesser degree as you soar along it. One "beat" will be slow relative to the ground as you pull into wind and the other very fast. Be careful to maintain airspeed on the fast leg! There are some other terms that are used in the sport and in this handbook — refer to the glossary at the end.

❻ Health and safety

Before you embark on a paragliding course the school will probably ask you to sign a form attesting that you will not drink, take drugs etc and also that you are of reasonably sound body (they seldom inquire after your mind!). Flying itself actually requires very little physical effort in most circumstances. However, to fly well does require reasonable reactions and, certainly during the training period, you do need to be able to climb a fairly steep hill several times.

People of a wide variety of ages and occupations enjoy paragliding but if you are daunted at the prospect of walking up a steep hill or have a history of epilepsy, heart complaints or other medical conditions, you should consult the school before signing up.

As a general rule the school will, in such instances, ask you to produce a doctor's note certifying that you are fit to fly. Many schools require a similar note for pupils aged 50 or more. The Air Navigation Order states that you may not be the solo pilot of an aircraft below the age of 16. Those aged 18 or less must have written consent from their parent or guardian. You will also find somewhere on your booking conditions that the chief instructor reserves the right to refuse to train anyone he considers unfit or ill-prepared to fly. The reasons are self-evident. The school's primary concern is safety.

Partial deafness is usually no problem, provided the instructor is informed (in one instance a student pilot did not mention the fact that he was deaf in one ear — unfortunately, the radio system being used at the time only had a speaker on one side of the helmet!).

Flying requires good visual awareness, both for setting up a landing at the correct position and altitude, and also for knowing where other pilots are when you are flying: it becomes second nature to keep a kind of visual map of the position of other fliers which is constantly updated by glimpses as you turn, and through your peripheral vision.

If your sight is OK with glasses, that is fine, as you can wear them with no difficulty (though some people use a cord or elastic to make sure they stay in place.) Contact lenses are less practical as they could fall out, and a heather-covered hillside is not a good place to look for them. Any permanent visual impairment may make you unfit to fly, and again the instructor will ask for a doctor's certificate before accepting your booking.

Clothing

In the summer months it is not unusual to see pilots flying in shorts and T-shirts. However, until you have amassed a good deal of experience it is better to wear something that offers more protection — it is quite possible that you will be falling over, or even being dragged along the ground. During your course you will be required to roll about on the grass or heather as part of your training, so do not wear anything that is too fragile or expensive! Gloves are invaluable as, even in summer, a good breeze on a hill-top can be cold, and when you are flying your hands are always in the airflow. A good wind-proof jacket is also essential in all but the best weather. If you are flying in winter, wear plenty of layers: it is easy to take things off if you've brought too much, and it can spoil your enjoyment and affect your concentration if you are shivering.

Footwear

Good footwear is essential: during training you will be walking up hills and a good grip is necessary. If your landings are less than perfect, the ankles are the first set of shock absorbers available so something offering good support is a good idea. Hiking or fell boots are fine. In any event, bring spare shoes as your flying gear may get wet. If you are serious about taking up the sport then there are some ideal boots that are light, waterproof and have good ankle support and grip, that are made especially for paragliding. They generally cost anything from £60 to more than £100 and most centres stock them. Boots with hooks can be a problem as the lines can become tangled in them.

Learning how to do it ❼

This is a brief introduction to the training system used at most approved schools in the UK. There will be some variations from school to school, of course, and in some countries the reverse launch that is used in windy conditions is not usually relevant. This syllabus refers to foot-launching. There are some other disciplines to be mastered if you are launching from skis, or being towed aloft.

Day one

It is usual to begin the day early by ringing the centre to check on weather conditions, and in some cases the meeting place. If you do not ring in, or if the school does not offer this facility, you run a far greater risk of a fruitless journey. Assuming the weather is fine, the instructor will begin by answering any question anyone may have and giving a brief chat on the sport. He or she will check that everyone is in good health and fit to fly, and ask if anyone has any other experience of flying or parachuting that could be useful.

You will be encouraged to ask questions. It is not the sort of class where you can sit quietly at the back and nod even if you do not understand something: your safety can depend on your knowing what is going on so that you can decide what to do next. You will be required to join the national association — this is mandatory in the UK as it confers third party insurance which is necessary before you fly. Some schools will also provide you with a theory booklet for you to use as a back-up to your instructor's lessons.

When you arrive at the slope, a few minutes is often spent assessing the site, pointing out the possible problems etc and checking the wind strength and direction. An introduction to the equipment and a demonstration of pre-flight checks come next. Your instructor will then usually demonstrate the appropriate take-off technique for the conditions, making it look very easy, of course. Now it is your turn: launch practice is usually done on flat or gently sloping ground, so you need not worry about being thrown off a cliff. Your altitude gain on the first few attempts is unlikely to exceed the length of your instructor's reach. Before you fly you will be required to master a parachute landing fall (PLF). It is quite usual for students to land on their feet every time, but safety is the prime consideration, and years of experience in the parachuting and parascending worlds have shown that the risk of injury if you should miscalculate your approach, or have some kind of emergency that means your landing is going to be fast or hard, is radically reduced if you are able to perform a PLF.

After lunch (not including alcohol) you will probably be doing a few longer runs, getting used to the controls and responding to the instructions. At first, the instructor will probably run beside you but then you may be responding to instructions from someone standing in front of you signalling with bats (rather like those used to signal jets on aircraft carriers). If it is windy you may be able to do this standing or lying in a stationary position, if not it will involve running down a gentle slope. Then it is on to

Ground handling and launch practice

"hops" — low flights with ground clearance of only a few feet initially, working up to longer and higher flights as your confidence and ability improve.

Over the next two or three days or so you should master ground-handling, often the hardest part to learn, become practised at pre-flight checks and flight-planning, and be achieving high solo flights including 180° turns. To achieve your Student pilot rating, you need to demonstrate that you can:

- Cope with your canopy both on and off the ground
- Assess the site and conditions
- Plan and execute flights, including flying at different airspeeds and making 180° turns and controlled landings.

You will also be required to pass a basic theory test. From then you are looking forward to soaring, landing back on the hill-top, thermalling and canopy instability exercises, logging some hours of airtime and gaining experience towards your higher proficiency qualifications, and joining a club. These are covered elsewhere in this handbook.

Site assessment

To assess when and where to fly you need to be able to visualise how the air is behaving: where will the good lift be? where will the wind be stronger or lighter? what is the likelihood of turbulence? To understand its behaviour we need to know a little bit about the air. Air is composed of molecules which are bouncing around all over the place, constantly colliding with each other and any nearby object. It has mass and weight, which is handy as it keeps the air stuck to the planet. We do not take much notice of the air in our daily lives unless the wind is very strong but, when flying, its behaviour is of crucial importance and absorbing interest. The air is gaseous, but it can be described as behaving like a liquid, so perhaps the easiest way to visualise its movement is by imagining it as water flowing over the landscape. Obviously, air can climb slopes more easily than water but it gives you the general idea.

When you stand on a hilltop with the air moving along as wind, try to imagine the flow as a river. Ask yourself where you would see rough or white water: in and around woods and buildings, in the lee of hills, wherever an obstacle interrupts the flow. *(See fig 10.)* We have immediately established the major areas of turbulence. The reason why air (like water) has a turbulent flow is because it cannot make sharp changes of direction. Its mass and velocity keep it moving one way. This analogy also explains some other characteristics of airflow that are important to us. A small or conical hill can not generate as much lift as a straight ridge as the air will flow round rather than over it if it can (rather like a rock in a stream). If you do have a long ridge but it has a gully or pass in it, *(see fig 11)* the air will

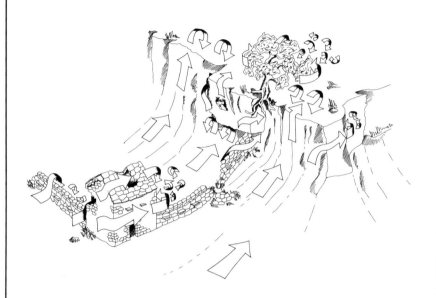

Fig 10. Common areas of turbulence

Fig 11. Airflow in a gully

Fig 12. Airflow at ridge ends

Fig 13. Airflow in a bowl

accelerate through the gap and so this area should be treated with caution. One pilot flying along a line of hotels on top of a coastal ridge in Israel flew too close to such a gap and described the experience as being "Hoovered" backwards through the space. He ended up on the roof of a house (which fortunately are flat in that part of the world).

The same phenomenon is found at the end of a ridge. *(See fig 12.)* The last few metres are often of no use as the wind is escaping around the end of the ridge rather than being pushed over the top as lift. In very mountainous areas, or those with narrow valleys, you may find that the airflow is affected more by the shape of the land than by the prevailing wind direction. *(See fig 13.)* Even in a light westerly breeze the wind in the bottom of a north-south valley will be northerly or southerly. If the wind is forced to change direction suddenly — by flowing over a cliff for example — the result of its inertia is to leave an area of relatively low pressure behind the obstacle. The air then curls back on itself to fill the space and the result is a rotating airflow or "rotor". Fig 10 shows such common areas of turbulence.

The advantages of all this are significant to the soaring pilot. When wind comes into contact with a slope it is forced upwards and the flow has a vertical component we call lift. The steeper the angle the air climbs at, the better the lift. A 45° slope with a given wind speed will always create less lift than a 70° slope in the same wind speed, as the vertical component is less. *(See fig 14.)*

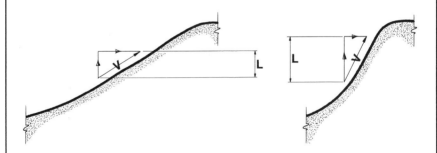

Fig 14. Steep and shallow slopes and the different amounts of lift(L) produced for the same wind speed (V).

We also need to take into account the wind strength and direction. Is it too strong? is there enough wind to soar? is it blowing directly onto the hill? Very often the wind does not meet the hill at a right angle. If it is, say, 30° "off" the slope, less lift will be produced as the air will climb the hill at a shallower angle. You will notice this as you climb the slope yourself! If the wind is "off" it also means that when you are soaring in the rising air in front of the slope, you will, on alternate beats, be flying on a downwind leg — more about this elsewhere in this handbook. You must make the decision whether it is worth flying or moving to another hill, or not to fly at all.

This kind of judgment can only be made with experience. If in doubt, do not fly. While assessing the site there are other factors to consider. There may be hazards such as power lines. The landing area should be large enough for your level of experience; and if you are planning to soar and top-land there must be a suitable area for this.

When you begin soaring you will be able to look at a site, know where the best lift is likely to be, where there is going to be sinking air and turbulence, and be aware of any hazards. This should give you enough information to decide if it is suitable for you to fly.

Wind gradient

Air is affected by friction as it moves over the landscape: all the grass and trees, bushes and buildings obstruct the molecules, preventing them from travelling the way they want and slowing them down so, at ground level where there is lots of friction, the air is moving relatively slowly. A few metres above the surface there is far less friction, though the air will still be slowed to some extent by the slower moving layer beneath. The higher you go, the less restricted and therefore the faster the wind will be.

At 300 metres or so above the terrain the relative drag decreases more slowly in most circumstances and the effect becomes less marked — *see figure 15*.

This gradient in windspeed is particularly noticeable on the hills we fly; the "normal" gradient of say 10mph in the landing field and 15mph at 100 metres above it is exaggerated by a related phenomenon — the 'venturi' zone. Paraglider pilots choose to fly ridges that offer the best lift, that is to say hills which the wind is forced to flow over.

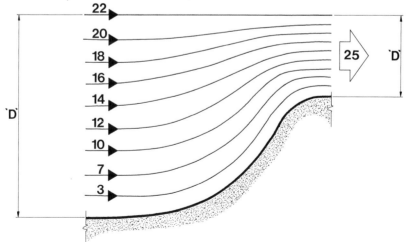

Fig 15: Wind gradient due to ground friction and venturi effect over the ridge crest (sometimes known as the 'compression' zone).

In addition to the wind gradient the airflow is accelerated over the crest of the hill by being squashed between the ground and the weight and inertia of the horizontal wind above it. The effect is the same as airflow over a wing — the less space there is, the faster the flow must be. The result of this is that, on a good ridge with a breeze blowing at it, there will be a kind of super wind gradient which can easily make the wind speed at launch two or three times that in the landing field.

It is vital to appreciate this for two reasons in particular. Firstly, if you launch from below the top of a hill, you must assume that the wind will be much stronger above you and if ascend into this stronger zone you could have a problem. The second is to do with flight planning. You may suddenly find that you are approaching the landing area more quickly than you anticipated, and with less headwind to reduce your groundspeed, your glide performance can improve dramatically. If you can anticipate this situation it is much easier to avoid an inadvertent stall by misjudging your speed, or an overshoot of your intended target.

⑨ Weather assessment

In addition to the properties of the site, we also need to know that the weather is suitable. The weather is a huge subject and there are some excellent books that are definitely worth reading if you wish to know more. To confine ourselves here to the fundamentals, we have three basic requirements.

Good visibility

It is self-evident that it is dangerous to fly if there is low cloud or mist obscuring the hill. Apart from the very real danger of it thickening suddenly and you becoming totally lost, it is quite possible that other aircraft could collide with you. If you are in cloud well clear of the surface then you run the risk of encountering both civil and military traffic flying on instruments. In any event, it is illegal to fly in poor visibility whether caused by cloud or darkness (see Air law, page 73).

Rain and snow

Flying in light rain or drizzle is miserable but it is not dangerous for short periods as long as the visibility is OK. It is often easier and quicker to fly down than walk if the weather turns poor. It is worth noting, however, that it means getting a nice dry canopy wet and it may be a long job to dry it out again. If there is heavy rain or snow it becomes very dangerous to fly. The reason is that the water or snow is carried into the canopy with the airflow and cannot escape. It will build up in the trailing edge and

Fig 16. Wind speed indicator

eventually it will distort the canopy and disturb the flight characteristics. If sufficient weight builds up you could enter a stall from which you cannot recover. One pilot has already been killed in this way flying in snow.

Wind

We require a reasonably smooth breeze to fly. For training, it can be anywhere between zero and about 16 miles per hour (though not too gusty). For ridge soaring we need at least seven or eight miles per hour, but no more than 20. We can check the wind strength and how smooth it is in several ways. The first and most important is by feel and experience. Standing on the edge of the hill for five minutes before deciding whether or not to fly is never a wasted exercise. If you think it is near the top limit for you this is particularly true: you would not wish to launch only to find that you had taken off during a temporary lull. You can confirm your impressions with a wind speed indicator. These come in several forms and give you an accurate read-out of the wind speed. They can only tell you what the wind is doing on the spot where you are holding them, so it is worth walking to the edge of the slope and angling them into the airflow to obtain the highest reading you can. This will be the most accurate. They can also assist in deciding just how gusty it is.

Gusts are the thing to watch out for: it is safer to fly in a steady wind of, say, 18mph (providing the site is suitable) than in one that is varying between eight and 16 mph. There are also visual clues to the wind's behaviour. Among the most obvious are windsocks or streamers (greatly underused in our opinion — every site should have one) and other pilots. You will often be sharing the site with hang glider pilots whose craft have a greater resistance to turbulence. If they are getting kicked about it is a good idea to wait a while. The best plan of action is always to ask those who have just flown (hang gliders or paragliders): they are usually happy to give you their impressions. Model aircraft and birds can also be useful indicators.

Clouds offer perhaps the best way to assess the wind from the ground. Look first at how quickly they are travelling; if there seems to be just a light breeze on the surface but the clouds are hurtling by only a few hundred metres above your head some further investigation is required before you consider flying. The other way in which clouds can help you assess conditions is that each cloud type is an indicator of the air's behaviour. Thermals — rising columns of warm air which create lift and associated turbulence — are frequently marked by cumulus (cotton wool) clouds formed when the moisture in the air condenses as it cools. Lenticular clouds are indicators of atmospheric waves set up by the flow of the air over hill or mountain ranges. Such waves are a source of both lift and, at their fringes, turbulent air. Perhaps the most noticeable of all clouds are cumulo-nimbus (cu-nimb for short) which are associated with heavy rain and storms and in which the turbulence has been known to tear the wings off sailplanes. *Thermals and wave lift are discussed in Chapter 27, Cross-country flying.*

The greatest single cause of accidents is flying in poor or unsuitable weather conditions (especially strong winds). If in doubt always ask for advice. Remember the mountains will still be there tomorrow.

⑩ The BHPA and the rating system

The British Hang-gliding and Paragliding Association is the governing body of the sport in the UK. The Civil Aviation Authority, which controls all non-military flying in Britain, has delegated to the BHPA the responsibility of ensuring adequate training, pilot and instructor qualifications, aircraft airworthiness and accident investigation. In addition to this the BHPA liaises with other air-users' associations and with land-owners, the government and the general public. It arranges insurance cover for members and publishes regular bulletins detailing safety notices and other information and the monthly magazine, *Skywings!* Together, these tasks represent a major undertaking and most of the work is done by unpaid voluntary officers. We shall only retain our enviable freedom to fly if the BHPA and its members can act, and be seen to act, responsibly. Most nations where paragliding is established have a similar association.

PRS PROGRESSION

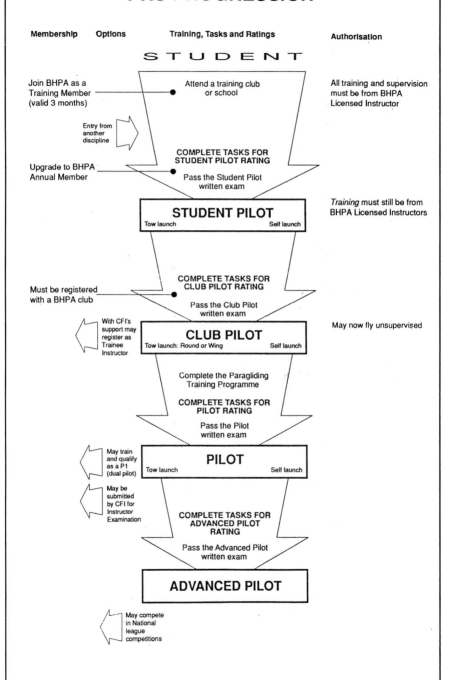

Membership   **Options**   **Training, Tasks and Ratings**   **Authorisation**

S T U D E N T

Join BHPA as a
Training Member ———————————●   Attend a training club
(valid 3 months)   or school

*Entry from
another
discipline*

All training and supervision
must be from BHPA
Licensed Instructor

COMPLETE TASKS FOR
STUDENT PILOT RATING

Upgrade to BHPA
Annual Member ——————————●   Pass the Student Pilot
                               written exam

STUDENT PILOT
Tow launch   Self launch

Training must still be from
BHPA Licensed Instructors

COMPLETE TASKS FOR
CLUB PILOT RATING

Must be registered
with a BHPA club ———————————●   Pass the Club Pilot
                               written exam

With CFI's
support may
register as
Trainee
Instructor

CLUB PILOT
Tow launch: Round or Wing   Self launch

May now fly unsupervised

Complete the Paragliding
Training Programme

COMPLETE TASKS FOR
PILOT RATING

Pass the Pilot
written exam

May train
and qualify
as a P1
(dual pilot)

PILOT
Tow launch   Self launch

May be
submitted
by CFI for
Instructor
Examination

COMPLETE TASKS FOR
ADVANCED PILOT
RATING

Pass the Advanced Pilot
written exam

ADVANCED PILOT

May compete
in National
league
competitions

ELEMENTARY PILOT RATING TASKS

The student must progress through Exercises 1 to 9 of the Training Programme and complete the following task to the satisfaction of the Instructor:
1. Demonstrate pre and post flight routines (eg inflation, launch and collapse drills).
2. Safely carry out launch assistant duties for other pilots.
3. Demonstrate pre-flight checks.
4. Complete:
a. for the tow student a minimum of 10 flights and attain self release from at least 300 feet AGL.

b. for the hill student a minimum of 3 low level flights, with a further 6 to at least 100 feet AGL.
5. Complete 4 appropriate controlled landings in a designated area.
6. Demonstrate safe airspeed control.
7. Demonstrate left and right turns.
8. Describe and evaluate a site and give a flight plan appropriate for the conditions.
9. Satisfy the instructor as to attitude and airmanship.
10. Pass the EP written examination paper.
NOTE: This rating is similar to stage 2 of the FAI Para Pro scheme.

CLUB PILOT RATING TASKS

The EP must successfully complete exercises 10 to 12 inclusive of the Training Programme. As training progresses the student should demonstrate the following tasks to the satisfaction of the instructor:
1. Complete:
a. for the tow student a minimum of 15 since achieving EP rating, all self release from at least 500 feet AGL.
b. for the hill student a minimum of 20 flights since attaining EP rating, to at least 200 feet AGL, with 2 flights of at least 5 minutes duration above take-off height.
2. Successfully complete take-offs in low level winds (below 5 mph) and high level winds (between 10 and 15 mph)
3. Demonstrate stable 180 degree turns.
4. Complete landings, as appropriate, in a designated area (not to exceed 20 metres radius).
a. for the tow student on a Round canopy the location as decided by the Instructor.
b. for the tow student on Wing canopy the location is to bet within 50 metres of the launch point.
c. for the hill student the location as decided by the

Instructor, but for 2 flights the designated area must be for top landing.
5. Complete the appropriate log book entries.
6. Display an ability to fly competently and safely in the company of others; maintaining a good look-out, complying with the Rules of the Air and exhibiting good airmanship.
7. Satisfy the Instructor as to the correct attitude to continue a flying career both safely and competently.
8. Safely demonstrate slow flight awareness and discuss the relevant symptoms and dangers. (WARNING: Deliberate stalls must be avoided)
9. Demonstrate, where appropriate, safe and effective use of the 'Big-ears' rapid descent technique.
10. Maintain directional control whilst showing recovery from tucks of not less than 25 per cent.
11. Discuss and show an awareness of techniques for avoiding and recovering from tucks, stalls and spins.
12. Pass the CP written examination paper.
NOTE: this rating is equivalent to State 3 of the FAI Para Pro scheme.

PILOT RATING TASKS

1 a. for tow pilots — complete a minimum of 50 flights since achieving CP rating, with at least 30 flights to above 800 feet AGL in wind speeds of over 10mph.
b. for hill pilots — complete a minimum of 50 flights since attaining CP rating, with at least 15 flights to a height above take-off at least 15 flights in wind speeds of over 15 mph and at least 5 flights in thermic conditions.
2. Demonstrate controlled 360 degree turns in both directions.
3. Complete at least 5 flights of over 5 minutes duration:
a. for tow pilots — from a line not exceeding 600 metres, or the equivalent winch tow height.
b. for hill pilots — at least 5 minutes are to be above take-off height: additionally the hill pilot must complete a minimum of 25 hours flying since achieving CP rating.
4. Fly with proper regard to the Rules of the Air and Air Traffic Rules.
5. Complete 5 controlled landings in a designated area (not to exceed 10 metres radius).

Additionally the hill pilot must carry out 2 top landings at each of 2 sites.
6. Experience flying in four different wind directions and at two sites.
7. Display an ability to fly competently and safely in the company of others; maintaining a good look-out complying with the Rules of the Air and exhibiting good airmanship.
8. Satisfy the Instructors as to the correct attitude to continue a flying career both safely and competently.
9. Safely demonstrate slow flight awareness and discuss the relevant symptoms and dangers. (WARNING: Deliberate stalls must be avoided)
10. Maintain directional control whilst showing recovery from tucks of not less than 50 per cent.
11. Discuss and be able to explain the techniques for avoiding and recovering from tucks, stalls and spins; and emergency rapid descent techniques (B line stall and spiral dive).
12. Pass the Pilot written examination paper.

ADVANCED PILOT TASKS

To achieve AP rating the candidate must complete the following tasks:
1. Complete a minimum of 150 flights since attaining P rating.
2. Complete at least 35 hours since attaining P rating.
3. Achieve the FAI Bronze Eagle Badge (15km distance; 500 metre height gain *or* one hour duration).
4. Complete a 20km cross country flight.
5. Complete a 20km out-and-return flight.
6. Display an ability to fly competently and safely in the company of others; maintaining a good look-out, complying with the Rules of the Air and exhibiting good airmanship.
7. Satisfy the Instructor as to the correct attitude to continue a flying career both safely and competently.

8. Safely demonstrate slow flight awareness and discuss the relevant symptoms and dangers. (WARNING: Deliberate stalls must be avoided)
9. Demonstrate safe and effective use of rapid descent techniques (B lines and spiral dive). NOTE: If performed over land this manoeuvre is to be carried out using only specified gliders which have proven good recovery characteristics.
10. Demonstrate safe and effective recovery from a flat spin.
11. Demonstrate safe and effective recovery from an amplitude max spin. NOTE: Tasks 10 and 11 must be carried out over water with a recovery boat in attendance and with the pilot wearing a buoyancy aide and reserve parachute.
12. Pass the AP written examination paper.
NOTE: This rating is similar to Stage 5 of the FAI Para Pro scheme.

Parachute landing fall

A paraglider is unlike any other aircraft in that it offers no protection at all to the pilot in the event of a hard landing or crash. If you do approach the ground too fast or in the wrong direction it is certain that you are going to be the thing that hits it hardest. There are a couple of things we can do to protect ourselves: the first is always to wear sensible clothing, boots and a helmet. The second is to become proficient at the parachute landing fall. The PLF, as it is usually known, was developed in the UK by the military when the number of injuries sustained by paratroops on landing was becoming a cause for serious concern. There is no doubt that the technique has subsequently saved many potential injuries in the parachuting world. It works equally well for us, and for this reason it is a mandatory part of the BHPA's training programme.

The PLF works by reducing the shock to any one part of the body by ensuring that the shock is absorbed over a large area. A PLF can not be learnt from a book but the basic position and the roll are illustrated here. The important points to remember are—

- Tuck in your elbows and chin
- Bend your knees and keep them together
- Bend slightly at the waist
- Twist away from the direction of travel (45° or so is best)
- Try to go "floppy" (blowing out your air and "deflating" may help
- PRACTISE — it's no good if you can't remember what to do when the ground is coming up too fast.

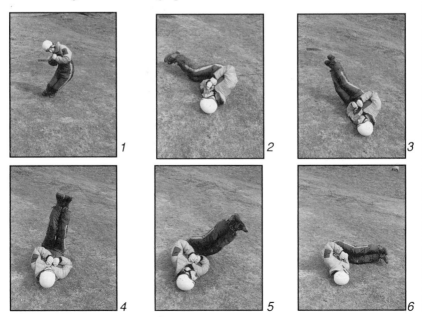

33

Common faults include:
- Not bending at the waist enough (the feet do not end up going the right way if you do this)
- Not turning as you flop: the sides of your knees, not the front of them, should touch the ground
- Being too stiff. Try to "crumble" into the ground, not fall over like a felled tree. The calves should touch first
- Legs coming apart as you roll — don't. Gripping something like a glove between the knees may help you practice.

In conclusion, the PLF is rarely used in a real situation but when it has been, it has certainly prevented injury. It should be practised regularly. If you can not remember anything else, always twist away from the ground, so you do not hit head-on, and bend — the foetal position will do the job.

⑫ Pre-flight checks

Like any aircraft, a paraglider must be pre-flighted before launch. The reason is very simple: the air itself is not inherently dangerous but it is very unforgiving of mistakes. The consequences of failing to do up a buckle are liable to be a lot more serious than falling off your windsurfer.

Pre-flight checks fall into three categories:

Canopy inspection.

To be carried out at least once a year or after any damage. Check all the fabric for tears and excessive wear; all the lines of stitching; all the lines including attachment points. **THIS INSPECTION SHOULD TAKE AT LEAST AN HOUR IF DONE THOROUGHLY**. If the canopy is faded it may be suffering from ultra-violet degradation, particularly in hot climates. If you are in any doubt have it professionally checked.

Daily inspection

To be carried out each day before flight.

Harness: Check stitching. Check for wear, especially where any metal touches webbing. Ensure buckles are done up correctly — it is possible to misthread some types. *See fig 19*

Maillons/karabiners: All should be fully done up (large and small). Note that all maillon gates should be exposed. *See fig 17*

Risers: Check stitching, especially where it is "bar-tacked", as this is very prone to abrasion. *See fig 18*

Control lines: Are they secured correctly to the handles? Do the last two metres show signs or wear? Make sure they are free-running and not wrapped around the risers.

Pre-flight checks are vital — for the first few days your instructor will double check for you.

Liz Addy

R. Cruickshank

The smile says it all — Fiona after her first paraglider flight.

35

Liz Addy

Checking the sky before take off

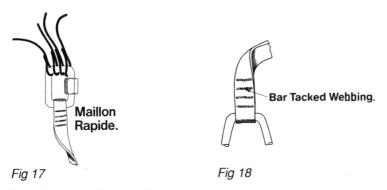

Maillon
Rapide.

Bar Tacked Webbing.

Fig 17   Fig 18

Pre-launch inspection

To be completed before committing yourself to each flight:

Harness: On correctly? Leg and chest strap(s) done up?
Helmet: Correct size and done up ?
Canopy: All cells fully inflated ?
Lines: All clear ? No tangles, no line-overs?
Controls: Functioning? No twists or tangles? Free running?
All clear: Is the space you are about to launch into clear of all other aircraft. Check in front, above and behind.

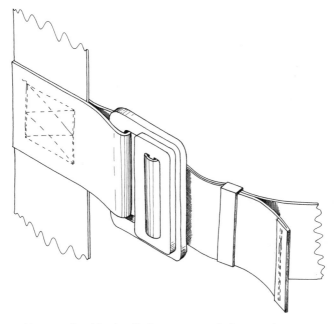

Fig 19. Harness buckle detail shown correctly fastened

37

Instructor Sue Larkin assists a student with a forward launch

A good snatch launch, notice that the pilot is checking his canopy without breaking stride

A harness showing cross-bracing arrangement restricting weight shift but adding stability. (S . Fenwick)

The forward (Alpine or Snatch) launch

⓭

Introduction

This method is used if there is a light (less than 8mph) wind or no wind at all. As the name suggests, it is commonly used in Alpine countries where the majority of launches are on slopes with little wind. It can be used in stronger winds if an anchor-man is used to hold the pilot while the canopy rotates up.

Preparation

Do your pre-flight checks. In no wind, or on flat ground, you may need the help of a fellow pilot to hold up the centre of the trailing edge. Make sure you have enough room to have a good run and check the canopy before you are committed. If launching from an area with rocks or vegetation that could snag a line, place all the lines on top of the canopy and stand with your heels touching the trailing edge. Take care not to stand on the lines.

1. Lay out the canopy flat on its back (top surface) with the trailing edge into wind.

2. Stand with your back to the canopy, facing into wind.

3. Hold the control handles as you would in flight and allow the rear risers to drape over your forearms or shoulders (you may need to hold the front risers in your hands as well). *See fig 20.*

4. Step forward until the "A" lines are fully stretched and evenly tensioned, check the air to make sure it is clear.

5. Run strongly and smoothly forward — keep your head down and lean forwards. If you are holding onto the front risers, let go of them when the canopy is almost overhead (you can feel the rearwards pressure reducing).

Leaning forwards helps your hands follow the natural arc of the front risers — do not pull them down or push them forward. The power should come from your run, not your arms.

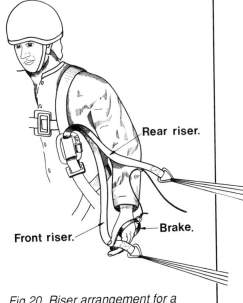

Rear riser.

Front riser.

Brake.

Fig 20. Riser arrangement for a snatch launch

39

6. Tilt your head back and check the canopy — cells open? lines clear? Try not to break stride or slow down as you do this: the more pressure and speed you can maintain the better. If a cell or two are collapsed on one side give a firm pump with the control on that side to reinflate them, do not launch with collapsed cells.

7. If you have time, you can double check that the controls are running freely. Apply pressure to the controls smoothly and evenly as you clear the edge of the hill.

⑭ The reverse launch

Introduction

The reverse launch is used when there is a breeze that can support the inflated canopy without the pilot needing constantly to move forwards. This is usually the case when attempting to ridge soar on hills rather than mountains. There is more to do, and therefore more to go wrong, but with some breeze there is also more time to play with and you can inspect the inflated canopy at leisure before deciding whether to fly. It is easier to pull the canopy up without falling over when you are facing it, so this type of launch allows you to manage alone in a wind that would require help if you were Alpine launching. However, if you have any doubt about your ability to control the canopy in a good breeze it is wise to ask another pilot to act as your anchor man and hold you while you inflate your paraglider.

Preparation

Do your pre-flight checks. Ask for an anchor man if required. Make sure that there is plenty of slack in the lines as you prepare, and put on the harness — it is pretty embarrassing to be dragged along with only one leg in the harness!

1. Lay the canopy out flat on its back in a gentle arc with the trailing edge into wind.

2. Stand with your back to the wind, facing the canopy. To do this you will have to lift one complete set of risers over your head. You should now have the risers crossed in front of you. *See Fig 21* — look carefully at which way they are crossed. If you decide at the start of your flying career which way you will turn, and do it the same way every time, you are less likely to get it wrong.

3. Grasp at least a metre of control line in each hand (do not cross your arms, just take the line that is controlling the same side as your hand). There should still be no tension on the rest of the lines at this point.

4. Without letting go of the control lines, hold the corresponding front risers in each hand as well.

5. By pulling on the front risers, inflate the cells to form a "wall"; if it is uneven or tries to lift too soon, you can alter its shape, or lower it, by

R. Cruickshank

A snatch launch. In this case the canopy was not laid out in an arc and as a result the tips have inflated faster than the centre.

Northern Paragliding

Rob Cruickshank 'anchors' a pilot reverse launching in a fresh wind.

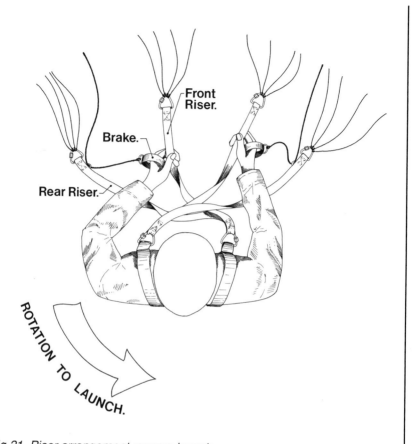

Fig 21. Riser arrangement reverse launch

pulling on the trailing edge with the control lines. If you need to lower the wall quickly, walk towards it at the same time. Ideally, the centre of the wall should be higher than the tips. A low wall of 2-3ft high is adequate in fresh winds, you will need a larger one if the wind is light. If the cells are squashed on one side it means the wind is coming from that direction and you need to move the wall round a few degrees until it is inflated evenly.

6. If all is well you can fully inflate the wing by pulling on the front risers. What you do with the control lines depends on the canopy you are flying.

If it is a modern intermediate or a performance canopy you will need to drop the metre of line, but hold the handles and keep them in your hands as you pull up the paraglider. Release the front risers when the canopy has almost reached the top of its arc above you. If it is still going strong and there is a danger of it flying right over you, stop it by applying some brake. Some models need only a touch to stabilise them, others need bucketfuls — you'll soon know your own.

7. When the canopy is stable above you, check for full inflation, clear lines etc. You can then either turn and launch immediately, or remain facing the canopy while you feel the wind, or wait for an opportune moment to turn and launch. You can steer the canopy in this position as if you were flying. Look over your shoulder to check there is no traffic before launching.

8. Turn to face into wind. Take care not to reduce the pressure on the canopy — it is common to collapse it at this stage by stepping back under the wing as you turn. An effective

"...and fly off as if that's what you meant to do all the time..."

technique is to reach out behind you with one leg as you rotate so keeping your movement constantly into wind. Before you turn, check the risers again: you need to follow the lower one round. If you have been holding the controls you will need to swap them into the correct hands at this stage.

9. Apply pressure smoothly and evenly to the controls as you clear the edge of the hill.

NOTE — you may find that you have turned the wrong way and the risers now have a 360° twist in them. If you are on the ground you can simply go round the other way. If you have been lifted off, as can happen on slopes, do not worry. Simply continue to use the controls to fly the canopy away from the hill until you are well clear. If you then let go of everything the risers will naturally untwist themselves. Once sorted out, reach casually for the controls and fly off as if that was what you meant to do all the time.

Cross brake launch ⓯

Many pilots prefer to use the cross-brake launch which is particularly useful when launching from a slope and there is a chance you will be lifted off as you inflate the wing. Or if you have a high performance canopy that is awkward to launch without applying brake throughout the launch procedure.

This is simply a reverse launch holding the correct control in each hand. There is a slight anomaly to get used to if you have previously used the other technique in that your left hand will be controlling your right tip and vice versa whilst you are facing the canopy. However it does mean that during the pull up and rotate sequence you have good control of the wing at all times. It is also a great deal safer should you be lifted off the ground during whilst still facing the wing.

The technique is simply to take the brake controlling the left tip (as you face the wing) in your right hand and vice versa. To do this one hand will have to reach under the crossed risers to reach one of the brake handles and the other hand will have to reach over them to reach the other. You can then pull up the front risers any way you wish. Most people find it easiest not to cross their arms but to pull up the left riser with their left hand.

You will notice that one brake line appears wrapped around the riser set as you are preparing to launch. This is quite normal and will untangle itself as you rotate. If you experience difficulty following this technique it is demonstrated in the *Touching Cloudbase* video.

 # Troubleshooting

Launches

Canopy will not climb overhead.
a. Too much wind? — try reverse launch.
b. Not enough wind? — try Alpine launch.
c. Have you remembered to drop the control lines before reverse launching?
d. Trimming devices (if fitted) — are they on too slow a setting?

Canopy tucks (collapses forwards).
a. Is there enough wind? — try Alpine launch or run faster.
b. You may need to be adding brake if the canopy is overflying you.
c. Pulling on the front risers too long?
d. Are you stepping towards the canopy when rotating and thereby reducing pressure?
e. Try pulling the canopy up holding the A and B risers together in your hands.

Canopy slews to one side.
a. Turbulence in launch area?
b. Canopy not laid out neatly?
c. Canopy not laid out into wind, or not running into wind?
d. Uncommitted launch — insufficient pressure.

Canopy collapses in the centre (claps hands).
a. Poorly laid out? — try laying it in a tighter arc.
b. Uncommitted take off.
c. Uneven ground? — try using a helper to hold up the centre of the leading edge.
d. Wing-tip holders helping you? — use one only, in the centre.

Ground handling

Many pilots find that the hardest part of paragliding is controlling the machine while still on the ground. The reason for this is that when flying, your weight will automatically swing below the canopy and except in turbulent conditions there will always be a load on the lines. On the ground however the canopy can slide over to one side of you or the other; it can drop behind or in front of you and the load can vary from moment to moment. The more you can minimise these variations the better the canopy will behave.

To keep the paraglider above your head in the proper position you will often need to use the brakes and sometimes the risers as well. A lot of problems can be eliminated by good preparation, making sure the canopy is into wind, knowing which way you will need to turn during a reverse launch, etc. Treat the canopy as hostile! If you give it the opportunity it will try and drag you through the nearest cow pat or fence! You must stay in charge and not allow yourself to be pulled around. If this proves impossible then collapse it immediately and start again making sure you have an anchorman. Remember that until the wing is flying correctly above your head the controls will serve only to pull it down further, not as effective steering devices. If it is well off to one side you may need to walk back under the centre as you brake or use the brake and front riser from the high side to pull it back up to the correct position. The other way you can help yourself is by keeping the load constant. This often means that you must correct and check your canopy while running or walking (often backwards) to maintain pressure through the lines. Take care not to walk backwards over the edge of the hill by mistake! Many people actually find it easier not to look at the canopy once they have rotated ready for launch. Try to develop control just by feeling what it is doing above you.

Inevitably sometimes you will lose the battle and the canopy will end up in a heap on one side or on top of you, and you will have to lay it out again. In a breeze you may find that a little careful manipulation of the brakes and risers can do this without the need to go and move the canopy by hand. An example of this is when the canopy has dived over and is "nose down" with the leading edge and cell entries pointing into the ground. It is often possible to lean back a little on the risers to give a pivot and with a long pull on one brake handle make the canopy fly back over into the correct starting position. Ground handling skills are very useful and are something that many pilots, eager to fly, spend too little time perfecting.

Now – Fix the bull with your eye – step back, and pass the handkerchief and the bull elegantly across the front of your body ...

"...your instructor may well be on the radio..."

⑰ First flights

By about the second or third day of training you will have completed several small flights. You should have mastered use of the controls and hopefully your instructor will have sorted out any bad habits (looking at the canopy as you fly along is a favourite one). It is likely that you have been responding to commands from the instructor or to "bat" signals from him as he stands in the landing area. Now you are ready for your first high flights.

"...a huge field with one tree in it..."

Flight planning

The higher you get, the larger the radius of the circle within which your possible landing sites will lie. Unless you are very lucky this means that you are now able to reach stone walls, barbed wire fences or the field with a bull in it. You can no longer simply wait for the ground to come up and meet you — this is where you start to really pilot the aircraft and make decisions for yourself. Your instructor may well be on the radio, but he will only be a back-up and he certainly won't be able to do anything if you do the wrong thing. The secret of being a good pilot is to think ahead. I have actually heard a pilot who said "well, I can console myself with the thought that the best pilot in the world could not have avoided crashing" (in a valley with trees, a river, a railway line and no landing area in it!) The answer, of course, is that the best pilot in the world would not have put himself in that situation.

The first point, then, about flight planning is that it includes planning not to fly. The next point is that you should think about any hazards and how you can avoid them before you take off *(see Chapter 8, Site assessment)*. This reduces your mental workload when airborne. The

Right: *Sequence showing reverse launch technique. The final picture demonstrates what happens when the canopy is allowed to overfly the pilot — a front edge tuck.*

third point about flying is that you must be prepared to revise your plan as you go along. If you decide to fly over that wall, and you start to sink low as you approach it, do not blindly follow your plan (or even your instructor's), decide on an alternative and do it. It is far easier if you think of these alternative flight plans, along with your intended plan, before you launch. The worst thing you can do is still be trying to make up your mind when you get there. I have seen pilots approach a huge field with one tree in it. They veer left as they come in , then right, then left again and narrowly miss hitting it through indecisiveness.

Exercises

People paraglide for different reasons. I am all in favour of having a go at something different — it's certainly more memorable than staying at home to wash the car. However, if you are interested in becoming a pilot, the best way to progress is to learn as much as you can from each flight. It is easy to waste a lot of time (and money) by flying with no eventual aim.There are several exercises you can set yourself, or your instructor can set for you, to make the most of each day.

Ground-handling. If the weather is poor — mist on the hill, for example, or strong winds at launch — you can still learn a good deal by practising your ground-handling and emergency collapses. PLFs can be done without even getting your paraglider out.

Launch practice. Many people find flying easier than launching. You can practise this on a small slope and fit in as many launches in a hour as you would get in a day on a large hill.

Rear riser steering. Pretend you have had a control line break. You can steer by pulling on the rear risers. DO NOT PULL DOWN ON BOTH REAR RISERS AT ONCE — YOU CAN ENTER A DEEP STALL. See *Chapter 29, Canopy instability exercises*.

Short field landings. This is an excellent one to practise — imagine an obstacle such as a fence across your usual landing area. Try to plan your flight to land short of it. When you have done it with an imaginary fence a few times, a small field with a real fence is far less of a problem.

Spot landings. As above, but try to hit a specific target — you learn a lot about yourself as well as about the capabilities of your wing. Don't forget, it is an exercise — it's not much use claiming from your hospital bed that you were the closest.

Slope landings. You may need to land on a slope one day and it is often a useful technique when you do not want to end up with a very long walk. This involves landing cross-wind — which is likely to mean faster — so start on a gentle incline and work your way up. Do not try to land on a slope of more than about 45° or in a strong wind. You could partly collapse or stall the canopy then find yourself airborne again.

360° turns. This is very useful skill to perfect as it will come in handy later for top-landings, flight-planning, and thermalling. You need a good deal of room for this manoeuvre as you will be flying downwind at some point. It is best at first to try when on a large hill with little wind.

Soaring beats. This is perhaps the most valuable of all the exercises — in order to prepare yourself for soaring flight, try to fly parallel to the ridge, execute an efficient 180° turn and fly back over the same ground in the opposite direction. If you can do this in light winds near the hill, or in stronger winds further out beyond the lift band, you will find doing it when there is lift is far easier.

⑱ Landings

Preparation

First you must decide where to land. The earlier you think about this, the more options will be open to you. The landing field should preferably be a flat area with no obstacles, clear of any turbulent flow from woods or buildings or other hills. The bigger it is the better. Other factors to consider are animals or people in the area, how easy it will be to get out of (is there a gate?). Are there any power or telephone lines to avoid?

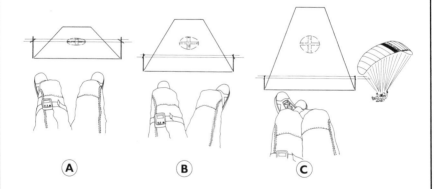

Fig 22: Relative motion: Flight A-B-C will clear the wires and land on the target. Flight C-B-A will land short.

Approach

Having followed your flight plan, you should be turning into wind at a minimum of five metres from the ground. Let the controls up if you have not done so already so that you are flying at maximum glide ($^1/_4$ brake position) or, in no wind, at maximum speed. Just before the touch down you need to flare by braking strongly and smoothly. The exact amount of brake is determined by the wind. If there is no wind, a full flare is required. If there is a breeze you will need less. Every flight is different and you will have to practise to discover exactly when, and how hard, you need to flare.

The major cause of problems with landings is that pilots seem to accelerate towards the ground on approach (due in part to the effect of wind gradient and in part to their reaction to the optical illusion created as the ground fills more and more of their field of vision). Some pilots' very natural reaction to this is to gradually brake more and more as they near the ground in an often sub-conscious attempt to keep their groundspeed low. The result, unfortunately, is that they can inadvertently stall too early and are "dumped" as the canopy stops supporting them.

A different problem is that some pilots lift up their legs as they come in. Your legs are your landing gear and much better equipped to withstand shocks than your backside. You need to make a conscious effort to sit up in the harness and actually reach down for the ground with one foot. If one foot touches first it is easy to run off any excess speed. If both touch together it gives a very neat landing if you have no forward speed. But, if you have, the next move is to fall over.

Touch-down

Once on the ground it is easy to relax, but the flight (and the danger of something going wrong) is not over until the canopy is safely wrapped up. If there is little breeze, the act of "flaring" the canopy to land will induce a stall as your feet touch and the paraglider will collapse onto the ground. To ensure it does not drape over you, it is wise to continue to move forwards and hold the flared position with the controls. This makes the canopy fall behind you and, by keeping the lines stretched, helps to prevent tangles occurring. It is only necessary to flare sufficiently to touch down gently and so, in a breeze, you may only need to brake gently. In this case, the canopy may remain inflated above you. There are several options open to you at this point. With some practice you can turn to the reverse launch position and use the inflated wing to help pull you back up the hill.

You can continue to walk or run with it still inflated (provided you move more or less into wind). This can be useful if you have touched down in a muddy or rough area or if you need to clear the area for others coming in to land. If you wish to collapse the canopy the best method is to turn and adopt the reverse launch position and then flare while running towards the canopy. If the wind is strong, a very good way of collapsing the canopy is to pull down sharply on the rear risers. The method which offers the most effective means of "killing" a canopy that is trying to drag you is to turn and, releasing one control completely, run towards the canopy pulling the other control hand over hand. *More details of landing in strong winds and subsequent canopy control are outlined in Chapter 23, Top landing.*

A pilot's eye view from altitude. Note the accelerator stirrup in use.

• LEAVING SCHOOL •

After your student pilot's course

Once you have completed your initial course you have three options open to you. The first is to decide that this is not really for you, but you'll take your certificate home, thankyou very much, and hang it on the wall. The second option is to continue as before, working your way up to the next level as a club pilot, using the school's equipment. This will give you the opportunity to decide for certain you have found your vocation, whereupon you can consider buying your own equipment. If you follow this path you will still require further instruction, of course. The third option is to buy a canopy of your own. If you are to continue learning on your own canopy, you may be able to do so at a reduced cost. Whether you are using the school's, or your own, equipment you will now need to join the national association as a full member. You should also make contact with your local club as, once qualified, it is the club members you will be meeting out on the slopes. Most clubs run a variety of social events and have meetings each month or so, in addition to meeting when out flying. They may also publish a guide to your local sites showing their status and suitability, nearest phones, who to ask for permission and any hazards or rules etc.

Buying a paraglider /airworthiness classifications ⑲

The pace of paraglider development is very rapid and therefore it is impractical to refer to specific models in this section. However, there are a few questions that you should ask both yourself and the seller to make sure that you purchase the right product.

How much can you afford? When budgeting to buy a canopy remember that you must allow for a harness, a helmet and probably some extra training too.

How much do you weigh? It is very important that you get the right size — too large and it will be slow and may behave badly in turbulence. Pilot weight is a vital factor in determining stability. Too small, and it will have a poor sink rate performance making soaring difficult.

What sort of pilot are you? Some wish to float around on pleasant days; others are keen to get the maximum performance and are aiming for cross-country or competition flight. In broad terms, you have five choices.

Used intermediate machines

There is a huge range of models available, ranging from very basic designs which have dreadful performance by current standards, to some excellent models that have only recently been superseded. Avoid wings more than about four years old as their useful life will be fairly limited. Signs of obsolescence are only two risers and no facility to big ear (a very important safety feature) and no accelerator system. Prices tend to be very low, but this may be a false economy as the resale value in a year or two is likely to be next to nothing, and in the meantime airtime will be more difficult to achieve.

Pros Price

Cons Depreciating fast, harder to soar, may be worn out

Used high performance machines

Performance may be good but many are completely unsuitable for inexperienced pilots. This sector of the market is a real minefield, with some wings having rather nasty habits that may have been acceptable to the hot-shot first owner but may be unacceptable to you. If you are a first time buyer do not even consider something with two or more B ratings or a C rating in its ACPUL test. Do not consider one of these unless you really know what you are doing.

Pros May be cheap. May look good

Cons Everything else

New intermediates

A couple of years ago intermediate meant a 35 cell wing with all As in its ACPUL certification, with easy handling and moderate performance. This group is still going strong and some good wings fall into this category. They are ideal for the recreational pilot and as this sector of the market is very price conscious they are usually good value for money. Newer models will hold the Standard ACPUL rating.

Pros User friendly, good resale value, fair performance

Cons No real cons except for the more ambitious pilot

Sport canopies

The term "Sport" has become widespread to describe the recent generation of high performance wings which, due to the evolution of design, are proving suitable for beginners to fly. Typically featuring 40+ cells and Standard rating in their ACPUL tests, these wings represent the largest and fastest growing sector of the market, perhaps because they appeal to more experienced pilots and beginners alike.

Pros Very good performance, will last you a long time, good resale value

Cons No real cons, some may be pricey

Top performers

The state-of-the-art canopies as used by competition and experienced cross-country pilots, these wings represent the cutting edge of paragliding technology and deliver excellent performance particularly in glide and speed range. They are not suitable for first time buyers with even the more docile models needing some expertise to fly well if the air should be turbulent. A few may require a great deal of skill to fly safely. Usually "Competition" rated, though some may feature "Performance" ACPUL classification, this does not mean they are suitable for inexperienced pilots. If you do have plenty of experience and are seriously competitive, then of course you have got to have one!

Pros State-of-the-art performance

Cons Requires expertise to recover well from unstable situations. Price/resale value may drop sharply and hard to sell when superseded

General pointers

If you can afford to buy new, that is usually the best policy. The new canopies are an order of magnitude better than even two year old ones. Not only do you get more flying because of this, but it may well cost you less in the long run as older canopies depreciate very fast. The exceptions are of course if you can find someone who has quickly got bored, or moved up, and has a "nearly new" machine, or an ex-demonstrator etc. When buying new, always buy from an approved dealer: your instructor may well be the best choice (providing he is offering a good range of products — some schools are tied to one manufacturer and may sell that model even if it is not necessarily the ideal one for you).

It is often possible to get reduced cost training to soaring standard if you purchase a canopy from the school and fly on your own machine. Buy the right size: you will regret it if you do not. This especially important if buying secondhand.

Get a harness you know you are comfortable with: your dealer should advise you. Never buy used without first seeing the canopy flown and secondly flying it yourself. Always get a second opinion if it is a private sale. If the dealer or seller is not a competent pilot then his advice is not going to be worth much. Do not buy a canopy that has been repaired or modified unless you are 100 per cent satisfied about its history, who did the repair and that the manufacturer approves of any modification. NEVER buy a canopy without certification.

Airworthiness testing and classifications

Very few canopies are still available new that have not been submitted for an airworthiness test. Most of the reputable manufacturers display a classification by an independent body on their products and advertisements. The major European systems are the Guteseigel (German) and the ACPULS which is (apart from in Germany) universally accepted. Hopefully all major manufacturers will soon conform to the now internationally recognised ACPULS classification system. One of the commonest questions asked by students and of course first-time buyers is "What does the test actually do and what do the classes mean?".There are a number of routines through which the test canopy is put and its reactions noted by the pilots and by a panel of judges from a high-definition video recording.

The ACPULS certification is designed to be as objective as possible, the glider passes each test or it does not. The results are recorded in the user's manual and on a sticker fixed to the glider so that the pilot is able to be fully aware of the results. The system is far from perfect, it does no more than approximate how the wing will really behave in turbulence and it does not measure the ease with which the collapses or spins etc can be induced. Some canopies can pass, and have passed, all the tests with an "A" or a performance rating but may still be unsuitable for beginners. The first test is a load test. The wing is steadily loaded to eight times the maximum recommended weight (8G) this is done by pulling it behind a truck. Secondly the canopy is laid out again but this time with a slack line and a 6g weak link in the system. The truck accelerates away and the canopy is snatched with an instant 6g load. It must pass these tests with no failure. In the second part of the test the glider is put through a range of manoeuvres by a test pilot.

The tests are constantly being evaluated and new exercises are added or existing ones altered as necessary. *See Chapter 40*

Airworthiness classifications

Guteseigel 1 and 1/2. To gain these German classifications the canopy must have convinced the test pilot that it is forgiving and easy to fly, and is therefore suitable for a beginner. The nearest equivalent in the ACPULS system is giving a canopy Standard rating or all "A"s under the pre-94 system. There is a disadvantage to the German system in that it is not filmed and is purely down to a single pilot's skill and intuition. A different pilot could have a different opinion. The disadvantage of the ACPULS system is that while it is fair and the film can be re-examined by a panel, it does not give any indication of "feel"— some canopies for example may tuck or spin very easily but still recover in four seconds. The panel has no option but to award an A in these cases. It is also worth remembering that the ACPULS tests only assess recovery, not how easy it is to tuck (for example) in the first place. In fact some machines with a higher rating are harder to collapse than some with a lower one. A paraglider with

ACPULS certification carries an information label, an example of which is reproduced on page 129.

The result is that it is very difficult for the pilot to make an informed decision about the suitability of any particular model. It is not unknown for a canopy to pass an ACPULS test but fail the more subjective Guteseigel test. Fortunately there are moves towards amalgamating the two systems in an overall European standard. We can only hope that the best of each system is retained to give both objective and subjective results.

NB: When referring to recovery times bear in mind that the canopies are tested in ideal condition (still air) by highly skilled test pilots.

Additional equipment

(20)

Harness

Do not buy a harness with no seat. These were designed for short descending flights in the early days of the sport and are very uncomfortable for soaring flight. Make sure that you can sit back comfortably on the seat without undue problems. The better designs have leg-straps appearing from at least half-way back on the seat. All modern harnesses are adjustable — make sure that you are comfortable, the straps do not slip off your shoulders and that you are not uncomfortably upright or too supine. The attachments for the risers should be at least 6mm stainless steel and Maillon Rapide quick links. Climbing karabiners are also suitable, but perhaps the best option are small carabiners made specially for the job. These are available from most good dealers.

Most good harnesses offer the facility to fly "cross- braced" and it is strongly recommended that you fly with them set up this way for the first few hours by tensioning your waist strap or attaching a cross bracing element. (See photo page 38). Another useful feature is the ability to mount a reserve system neatly in the harness, check that the reserve handle is going to be visible and easily reached when fitted. A good reserve container should be closed with one or more curved pins, systems relying on velcro alone are no good. Some models have clear "windows" so that you can check the pins without disturbing the container. One other important consideration is back protection. A number of harnesses on the market feature some kind of protective back plate that is designed to prevent spinal injury in an emergency situation. These range from foam pads that are good at shock absorption but not so effective at penetration resistance to kevlar or polycarbonate plates that act as a shield against point injury from branches or rocks. What type of protection you need depends on what type of accident you are going to have!! Your first priority is likely to be absorbing shock, but if you can afford it you are best off with a hard plate together with a thick foam or polystyrene insert which will do both jobs. The latest trend is to incorporate some type of airbag system, the motor industry has already shown that these are the very best way to absorb shock in an impact. The type that is inflated by the pilot or by deploying a reserve also gives excellent protection of the upper leg area and the neck. (see photo left)

The disadvantage to all these protective devices is added weight and particularly bulk!

Helmets

Buy a good tested helmet. There are two main varieties: polycarbonate types frequently look like motorcycle helmets but with holes cut out over the ears to help you hear the wind-noise. These are excellent and afford the best protection, and are warm in winter. They are relatively heavy and can be rather hot in summer. Glass fibre climbing helmets are another option. They are usually adjustable to fit various sizes and are often used in schools. They are light and cool and leave the ears open. The protection to the sides of the head in particular is not as good as the previous type.

A more popular option these days is the "full face" helmet. Motorcycle types are completely unsuitable as they are too heavy and badly impair hearing. The lightweight types designed for paragliding are much better and of course do offer lower face protection. However, they have two potential drawbacks. The first is that in the case of injury they are much harder to remove without aggravating neck damage, and the second is that they may make it more difficult to perform mouth to mouth resuscitation. Types that have a detachable chin guard are now available, which can only be a good thing.

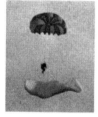

Many pilots choose to wear helmets made of plastic that are designed for use by cyclists. It is your head! If a helmet is damaged or struck hard, discard it as it reduces the strength considerably. Do not buy secondhand. Any helmet must be the right size and have no tendency to fall over your eyes.

Look for a CEN standard certification.

Right: Emergency parachute system being deployed. Pilot - Rob Cruickshank. (Apco Aviation Ltd)

Reserve parachutes

It may seem strange to carry a reserve system when we are already flying under a parachute. However, because our wings require constant air pressure to remain inflated they can be collapsed, either by excessive control movements by the pilot or by turbulence. In these cases, recovery is generally straightforward. However, there remains a possiblity of "wrapping up" the canopy to the point where it is impossible, or may take too long, to recover. We are not alone in the sky, and there is always a possibility of a mid-air collision, either with another canopy or (perish the thought) with something a lot heavier and faster. Reserves are rarely used, but it is a second chance. If you fly in a variety of conditions or with groups of other pilots, you may one day need it. They are mandatory equipment for cross-country or Alpine flying. A paragliding reserve is usually a small (24-35 sq metre) parachute.

Reserves are generally mounted in the rear of the harness with the deployment handle within easy reach. All the best ones have an airworthiness test (ACPUL or Guteseigel) and come with instructions for use and repacking.

A reserve should be mounted so that when it is opened the pilot is suspended by both shoulder straps.

Reserves must be aired, inspected and repacked at least every six months.

Parachutes are available in a large number of sizes and formats, these can broadly be divided into 4 types.

1. Hemispherical or tri-conical reserves

These work well and were very popular until four or five years ago. They require a relatively large fabric area and are correspondingly more stable in their descent, and somewhat slow in their deployment (opening) time. Perhaps the main reason they have fallen out of favour, however, is that they are quite bulky and heavy to carry around. These types are now mostly confined to the second-hand market in the UK.

2. Rocket deployed reserves

These are not a different canopy type but a different way of deployment. The rocket once activated can blast right through any paraglider fabric or for that matter several layers of hang-glider or microlight sailcloth and will stretch the lines of the reserve and speed up the deployment time significantly. If you are wrapped up in fabric, or need a very fast deployment (say near the ground) then this could be very useful. There are a number of disadvantages to this type of system however in that the weight and especially cost is greater, the rocket is a lethal weapon (actually some are modified military mortars) and could kill someone in a mid air collision situation or even if fired accidentally (ground handling in gusty winds for example). Another problem is commercial aircraft prohibit carrying devices of this type so you cannot take it on holiday with you, and finally they require expert maintenance to ensure they perform perfectly when you need them. Apart from certain specialist requirements like testing prototype wings for example, it is difficult to see the attraction of such a system. A recent trend has been to have a deployment system propelled not by explosives but by compressed air (available at any diving air station) and this must be a considerably safer option for those who feel they require such a system.

3. Reserves with drive

Some designs have slots in the envelope which give the reserve forward motion or "drive" these are for two purposes. The first is to aid stability by controlled bleeding of excess pressure and therefore reduce oscillation. The second is to allow the pilot to steer by converting the forward momentum into a turn using brake handles or weightshift through two or more risers. In order for the drive to work, however, the parachute must be allowed to fly correctly, a very difficult situation to achieve when a main canopy is flapping around behind it. Some reserves may be relatively unaffected by this (although you obviously cannot steer them without either dumping completely or at least wrapping up your main wing). Some reserves with drive actually fly just like the paraglider, and a likely result of deploying them is that the reserve will stall or fly away from the main (downplaning) which can cause a very dangerous situation — perhaps worse than that which caused the deployment. I have witnessed this happen to a pilot who threw a "square" reserve and who was very lucky to survive a 2,000ft descent of stalls and swooping dives as the main and reserve fought it out, taking it in turns to stall each other.

You cannot steer a reserve whilst still attached to an even partially-inflated paraglider — despite the misleading wording of some advertisements which may seem to imply otherwise.

4. Pulled down apex reserves

These are systems in which a central line holds down the Apex in a shape rather like an inverted saucer. This gives a relatively large flying diameter for relatively little fabric and therefore a good low sink-rate combined with a small light package. Another advantage is that these types operate at high pressure and therefore inflate very quickly — a great bonus as many deployments occur at a surprising low altitude (the commonest situation is a mid-air collision while ridge soaring). The pulled apex design does tend to oscillate more than a tri-conical or hemispherical type. Also, in the early days of paragliding the reserves went through a phase of being built very small indeed with correspondingly high sink rates. This was to a great extent due to the very optimistic 6.8m per second allowed by the German Guteseigel test — at that time the only recognised standard. Experience has shown that this is a rate that will give the heavier pilot a pretty fair chance of injury, and as a result the newer ACPUL test demands a sink rate of no more than 5.5m/sec with an 85KG payload.

Comparing reserves: a quick glance at the marketplace reveals that reserves are all different sizes yet sold for the same weight pilot! How can this be? The answer is that size (whilst important) is only one of the criteria in how well a reserve decelerates you. Flying diameter is actually a much better measurement as a plate could have a smaller surface area than a bowl yet have a greater flying diameter! In fact some shapes have better sink rates than others even with the same flying diameter. Another factor is fabric. Some reserves use more porous fabric than others (this is especially true of some German reserves) and so the reserve needs to be corresponding larger in order to have the same sink rate.

The UK is one of the very few countries that still does not insist on an independent test for reserves. However, I advise in the strongest possible terms that you ONLY purchase a reserve with an ACPUL or Guteseigel rating.

Instruments

It is perfectly possible to fly a paraglider well with no more equipment than your harness, helmet and senses. However, to use the available lift to its maximum potential, to thermal efficiently and to navigate cross-country you require some senses nature has not provided. The higher you are above the ground, the less reliable your senses become as the visual clues become less useful.

Variometer

A vario measures how fast you are rising or falling and displays this information as a sound, on a meter, or both. Most work by detecting changes in air pressure. A human can detect acceleration, such as flying into a thermal and shooting upwards, but smooth constant gains (or losses) of altitude are undetectable. Your senses can actually work to fool you. Lift of 500ft per minute may suddenly decrease to lift of only 200ft per minute. To the pilot this feels exactly the same as sinking at 300ft per minute and, without a vario, he may make a bad decision and leave the lift. A vario is therefore essential to know what is really happening.

Altimeter

An altimeter tells you how high you are above a specific pre-set point (see Chapter 25, Air law). You may think it is obvious how high you are, but until they have had a good deal of practice most people are amazingly bad at judging altitude, especially from great heights. Why do you need to know your altitude? There are three main reasons:

— Personal interest — "I made my best height of four grand today!" etc.
— To help you navigate your position relative to controlled airspace
  — are you under the Airway or in it?

— It complements the vario when thermalling. If you are flying in broken lift that is constantly up, then down, then up again it is soon impossible to know if you are gradually losing height or gradually gaining. An altimeter gives you this information at a glance. It could occasionally be of use in some competition tasks where you can work out beforehand that you can reach point B if you are at 3,000ft or better at point A.

In practice most variometers and altimeters are integrated units in one case. Most of these will give you very accurate information and allow you to switch between altimeter settings, for example you can check your height above take off and at the touch of a button check your altitude relative to airspace (see details of altimeter settings on page 82) many units will also remember details of your peak altitudes and other information from your last few flights. Some more sophisticated units function as a barograph, that is record a complete trace of your flight that can be down loaded into a computer or printer and which can form the basis of an official record claim.

All these functions have a use of course but only you can decide what is necessary for you.

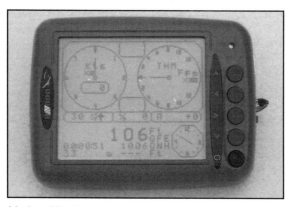

Vario altimeter

Compass

Useful for navigating — it is easy to get lost or disorientated after a cross-country flight involving several hundred circles over unfamiliar territory. Again, good navigation is required for avoiding airspace etc. It is a useful tool if you get caught in cloud, and invaluable simply as an aid if you get caught in the mountains on foot.

Barograph

A barograph is essentially an instrument that records a flight. This information is displayed as a trace which can be read to ascertain your duration of flight and also your altitude at any point during the flight.

Modern barographs are electronic and display this information as a print out, or by downloading on to a computer screen. Barograph evidence is a requirement for a flight to be recognised as an official record.

Map

Mandatory for cross-country flights. Rather than carry an air chart, a practical plan is to mark all the relevant parts onto an ordinary route-planner map. Good for finding your way back to the car too!

Radios

These must be airband in the UK and you may only use the specified channels unless you are licensed, maintain radio discipline and identify yourself in each transmission. Vox units are not usually a good idea as the microphone can be opened by wind noise, and it is easy to forget that it is on.

GPS (Global Positioning Systems)

Originally developed by the US military, the GPS system currently comprises 21 satellites whose relative orbits ensure that at least three are always above the horizon. The GPS units are small handsets that can plot a position from these satellites and so give a very accurate fix as to your position anywhere on the earth's surface. If enough satellites are above the horizon they can even give your altitude! A further facility is that you can program "waypoints" these are positions you can use as turnpoints or targets, the GPS can then advise you of the heading to take to navigate accurately to these points. These are very useful indeed for aircraft flying on instruments or for maritime traffic for whom accurate positioning is essential. The falling price of these units has meant that some pilots especially those undertaking long-distance flights over unfamiliar or featureless terrain, have found them irresistible as a safety and navigation aid. The fact that they can tell you exactly where you are, and therefore how far you have left to go, what your groundspeed is, and what heading to take to reach your goal; or even whether you've already broken that record before you've even landed are powerful incentives to own one! Just a note of caution however, a GPS cannot replace a map as it may offer a heading but it cannot inform you of hazards.

㉑ | Packing and care of your canopy

How you repack your canopy depends on what sort of terrain and wind conditions you are in and whether you have anyone to help you. You will need to decide which method is most appropriate to your situation. If there is any wind, your first move should be to orientate the canopy so that one tip is pointing into the wind. This makes it less likely to blow around while you fold it. Next, make sure the canopy is laid out flat on its back with no lines underneath it. Place all the lines on top of it (undersurface). Note — it is recomended that the harness is left attached and is thrown over so that it just clears the leading edge of the canopy: this keeps dirt and scuffing to a minimum, prevents lines becoming tangled and makes it easy to check that the harness is in the bag.

Fold the canopy as neatly as possible. If you are alone, or the terrain is rough and you do not wish to drag the fabric over the ground, this is best achieved by folding the tips into the middle; then each end to the middle again, and so on — *see fig 23.* If you have help you can either fold the canopy from each tip, one panel at a time, or concertina fashion, one panel at a time, starting at the centre and pulling each panel in as you fold. When the canopy is arranged as a double pile of folded panels press out the air trapped inside. This must be done working from the sealed trailing edge towards the leading edge where the air can escape easily through the cell entries. Fold one side onto the other and press out any remaining air in the same way, and fold from the trailing edge forwards. This should give you a fairly tidy package with the harness still attached, but not wrapped up in the fabric. Try to avoid carrying it around like this, as the bundle will inevitably slip apart. Always carry your rucksack with you so that you can pack the canopy up immediately.

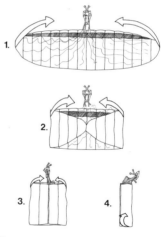

Fig 23. Packing a canopy

Care of the canopy

The fabric generally used for paragliders is prone to damage by repeated exposure to ultraviolet light, so do not leave it lying out in the sun for long periods. This is particularly important where the sun's rays are very intense, for example at high altitude or at low latitudes. The fabric and lines are of synthetic fibres and are easily damaged by heat. Take care not to smoke near them and never attempt to dry a canopy by applying direct heat. It is advisable to avoid getting the canopy wet but, of course, it sometimes happens. If so, dry it out fairly soon afterwards as it is possible to get mould or mildew on the fabric which can leave unsightly marks (paragliders dry in a matter of minutes in a breeze as long as water is not trapped in the cells).

Never store the canopy near chemicals or fuel as this could affect the material. If you are flying in a hot climate take care to pack your canopy into its bag and protect it from great heat. Canopies with Dyneema lines risk them shrinking if the temperature exceeds 100° C — this has happened where an unpacked canopy has been left inside a car. Never use chemicals to try and clean the fabric or lines: some cleaners that will remove oil will also attack the fabric (which is of course a by-product of oil). Sometimes, of course, paragliders do get damaged. If the damage is to the lines or a riser, or the webbing or metal of the harness, do not fly it until it has been professionally checked and repaired. If the damage is a small tear in the fabric of the harness, it should have no effect on safety. If the tear is to the canopy fabric it should be repaired as soon as possible. Minor tears, that is to say those less than 10cm long that are not on a seam or line attachment point, can be repaired using self-adhesive rip-stop tape. This is available in a variety of colours from camping shops and sailing equipment shops. If applying this kind of tape there are a number of pointers to get the best results.

1. The canopy must be completely dry and clean.

2. The tape should give a generous overlap around the damage.

3. The edges of the tear should be carefully aligned in their original position, otherwise there will be creases and additional strain on the area.

4. Always round off the corners of patches.

5. A patch should always be applied to both sides of the fabric.

6. The internal and external patches should be of different sizes to prevent stress lines.

7. Do not forget to make a special point of checking the repaired area as part of your pre-flight checks.

Lines also need maintenance — tests would indicate that they get weaker with use and at least one manufacturer recommends you change the main load-bearing lines (lower A and B) every 100 hours. As the canopy is groundhandled the lines do tend to get wet and dirty. This can have the effect of shrinking the outer sheathing of the line and so shortening it. As the A and B lines take much more load than the other lines, they may be stretched back again each time you fly. The results are self-evident, the canopy will fly at a higher angle of attack as the rearmost lines shrink the most. Stalls and spins become easier to induce and the top speed decreases. A moderate pull of 10-15kg on a line may reveal that they can be re-stretched by anything up to 2 or 3cm to achieve their proper length. If the lines appear excessively dirty, stretchy, or at all worn — replace them.

NEVER ATTEMPT TO REPAIR A LINE BY KNOTTING IT.

IF YOU ARE IN ANY DOUBT, SEEK PROFESSIONAL ADVICE.

Major damage should be referred to your dealer. All good dealers should be able to supply lines and other basic components. Apart from physical damage, canopies can be rendered unsafe through material degradation. The major cause of this, already mentioned in the section on fabric, is ultraviolet light. UV, a constituent of sunlight, gradually weakens the fibres of the cloth and prolonged exposure will make it increasingly porous and more prone to tearing. This problem is associated with a severe fading of the colours, so if your canopy appears very faded, ask a professional to check it for you.

Richard and Guy Westgate over Kuruman South Africa scene of their world record tandem flight.

Soaring flight

Soaring can be defined as maintaining or gaining altitude over a period of time without any outside input such as an engine or a tow-line.

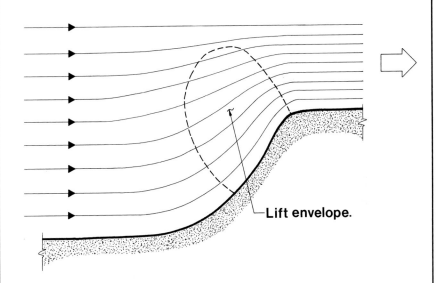

Fig 24. Section through ridge showing lift band

As we already know, a paraglider is just that — a glider. It must be gliding down through the air constantly to fly. So how can we soar? The answer is to find some air that is going up faster than we are going down. Let us assume your canopy sinks at about 300 feet a minute. If we fly in air rising at 600 feet a minute, after one minute we will have gained 300 feet of altitude. *(See Fig 25.)* Rising air is known as "lift" and there are several sources that a paraglider can use. The most common is ridge lift. This is produced when the wind is forced up over a ridge or cliff and forms a band of rising air we can fly in.

The other sources of rising air include thermals, wave and convergence. *These are discussed in Chapter 27, Cross-country flight.*

From what we know of site assessment and air behaviour we can visualise the "pressure wave" of air forming the lift band in front of the ridge. All we have to do is fly around in this area and we can stay up as long as we wish.This sounds very easy and often it is. However, it can require considerable concentration and effort to visualise and utilise this invisible force effectively. The best advice is to watch and learn from those who are already proficient. Birds of prey or gulls generally seem to have the right idea.

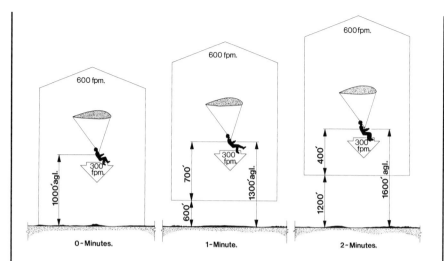

Fig 25. Flying down through a block of rising air, ie a thermal. The glider with a sink rate of 300fpm is flying through a block of air which is rising at 600fpm. The nett result after two minutes is a 600 ft height gain.

When soaring a ridge always make your turns facing into wind — *see Fig 26.* Try to follow a smooth extended figure-eight pattern, remember your site assessment and look for steeper sections of slope or those most into wind for the best lift.

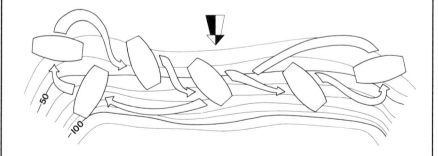

Fig 26. Typical "figure eight" soaring pattern

Hints

- Always try to turn in a lifting patch
- Watch out for gullies or the very end of a ridge where there may be no lift and you can be "hoovered" backwards
- The higher you get the further out the lift will extend — *see Fig 24.*

Top landing

So you are soaring. The view is wonderful and after a few minutes you can relax and concentrate on exploring the lift and perfecting your control. You are now ready to land back on the top (just think, no more long slog up that hill). First, look at the area you intend to land in. Is it suitable? Are there any potential hazards, has anyone parked a hang glider there while you have been flying? (most clubs have defined areas for landing that are kept clear if possible). If it is not a recognised landing area, could it suffer from turbulence or rotors? If in doubt, don't try it — land at the bottom. Ask other pilots and read your site guide to make sure it is advisable before attempting it.

If everything is OK, you need to plan your approach. You have three choices: track in from the left or right, or approach directly downwind. All three approaches end up, of course, with a turn into wind. For your first top landings a downwind approach is not usually recommended. So, left or right? If the wind is at 90° to the hill and the ridge is straight, the approach will be similar from either direction. Look at the area again, if you overshoot will it take you into the launch area or off the end of the hill? Choose the direction that gives the greatest margin for error — there are often unexpected patches of lift or sink above the top of a hill. Often the wind is not quite straight onto the face (see Fig 27). This makes the choice easier — track to the end of the downwind leg and start your approach from there.

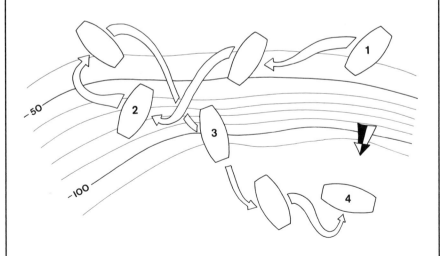

Fig 27. Top landing

L. Addy

Flying in paradise - Goa, India

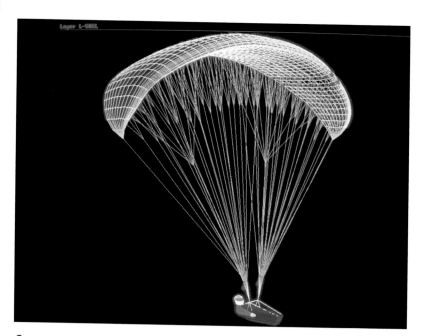

Computer aided paraglider design allows a designer's ideas to be calculated, plotted and cut in a matter of hours — see page 128. (NOVA)

1. Decide in good time that you are planning to top land (a good pilot always reads ahead). Do you have enough height? Do not assume that you will be lifted up as you approach the ridge, a painful collision may result if you do. Plan your turn carefully for the approach leg.

2. Commence your turn as you would if you were intending to carry on soaring then continue the turn until your track will crab you across the hill top. Be careful not to turn too much with insufficient height or you may not have room to turn back into wind.

3. Continue to crab until you are over your planned landing area then turn into wind.

4. As you turn into wind and begin to sink ease your brakes up then ease them down if you need to lose any excess speed. Do not forget that you will be landing in a reasonably strong breeze — something you may not have experienced previously, so feel your way with the controls. Do not flare hard unless it is obviously necessary. If, on your final approach, you find yourself too high, then a few gentle "S" turns will help you lose height. If in any doubt, overshoot and try again. With practice you will be learn to judge more accurately and be able to spot land in a small pre-determined area.

Touch-down and canopy control

Once your feet have touched the ground you have a choice to make. You may be able to "walk" the inflated canopy to a suitable area to pack it or to launch again, or you can choose to collapse it where you have landed — if there is only a light breeze you can collapse it as normal — *see Chapter 17, Landings*. If, however, there is a reasonable breeze your first action should be to release one control completely and turn to face the canopy, in this position you have far more control (as per a reverse launch) and you can see where the canopy will end up.

To collapse it, pull down hard on both rear risers, this will effectively stall the canopy and it will collapse. If the canopy is a simple two riser system then pull down hard on both controls and run towards it. In severe circumstances (you have fallen over), to prevent the canopy from dragging you, pull hard (hand over hand if necessary) on one control. This will cause the canopy to rotate and dive nose first into the ground. Once it is dropping nose first do not pull any more as it may go right round and fly back up again. It is very important, if you are doing these manoeuvres, that you should run towards the canopy at the same time to reduce the pressure. If the canopy dives into the ground with a good load through the lines to you, it may hit very hard and this could damage the internal cell walls. The more wind there is the more important that you run towards the canopy while collapsing it.

Occasionally you may find that the wind is strong enough to reinflate the canopy whenever you stop running towards it. In this case the only safe position is behind (downwind) of it. If you should find yourself landing moving backwards or in a gusty wind, sprint around to the back of the canopy as soon as it is down.Being dragged by a paraglider is an unnerving and potentially dangerous experience. If you should fall over and find yourself being dragged, try to roll onto your stomach so that you can see where you are going and again collapse the canopy by pulling one control hand-over-hand (until you get to the fabric if necessary).

 # Site discipline and rules of the air

Paragliders are subject to the same laws as any other aircraft *(see Chapter 25, Air law)*. But in addition to these there are some other disciplines that must be observed for us to be able to fly safely and without causing problems for others.

Sites

All land is owned by somebody, and before you fly from it you should find out whose it is and seek permission. Obviously, you must use common sense. If you are flying down from a remote mountain in the Andes it is unlikely anyone is going to worry. However, sites have already been lost by people flying in areas where grouse-shooting takes place or where there are sheep during lambing time. There is certainly nowhere in England or Wales that should be flown without permission. It is vital for the future of the sport that pilots follow sensible guidelines when out flying. These include:

- Keeping away from stock
- Not taking dogs onto hills where there may be sheep
- Not climbing over fences, walls or hedges
- Not lighting fires
- Closing gates
- Checking there is no shooting, or lambing (February to May)
- Parking sensibly
- Leaving no litter
- Flying with third party insurance, see below (and paying for any damage).

These rules are, of course, designed to help others. We also need to help ourselves directly by observing a sensible attitude on the site. For example —

- Do not leave equipment in the landing area
- Make sure everyone knows the site rules
- Offer to help to act as anchorman for other pilots
- Do not launch if the sky is crowded
- Always do a pre-flight check
- Only fly if you are in good health.

There are also some mandatory safety rules (failure to comply could invalidate your insurance, for example). These include —

- Wearing a suitable helmet
- Having the relevant qualification for the flying you are undertaking
- Being adequately covered by third party insurance (BHPA membership currently gives £1,000,000 cover)
- You may not fly when under the influence of drugs or alcohol
- Do not fly a modified paraglider or harness unless the manufacturer agrees to the changes.

Anti-collision rules

1. When approaching another aircraft head-on, break right. If this is impractical or unsafe because you are too near the ridge, allow the other pilot only to break — if you should go left while he goes right you are likely to collide.

2. When approaching another aircraft on a converging course the one on the right has the right of way (on your right — in the right).

3. Give way to pilots below you (they have less room to manoeuvre and may not be able to see you).

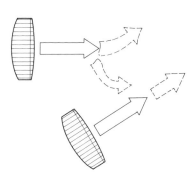

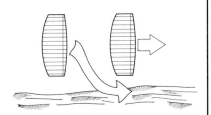

Head on collision situation — break right

Overtaking on a ridge — between the slower craft and the ridge

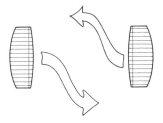

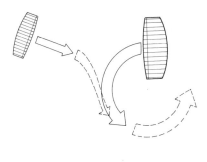

Converging — the craft on the right is in the right, the other must take avoiding action

Entering an 'occupied' thermal — turn in the same direction

4. When overtaking while ridge-soaring always pass between the other pilot and the hill. They are most likely to turn out from the hill so this reduces the risk of collision. It also prevents you from "cutting them off" from their landing area.

5. When in thermals always circle in the same direction as pilots who have joined the thermal before you. This means that your closing speed will be small and visual contact can be maintained.

6. Notwithstanding the above, it is the duty of every pilot to take any and every action necessary to avoid a collision. In other words, even if it is your right of way you are expected to take action if the alternative is a collision.

7. LOOK before you manoeuvre! (OK this is not the law- I added this one myself)- but I can tell you from my own experience and that of hundreds of our students, it's probably the most important of the lot! Manoeuvring includes doing almost anything, from letting go to scratch your nose, to taking off or commencing a turn.

Note — Because of the low relative speeds and the fact the pilot is exposed (not in a cockpit), it is often practical simply to shout at the other pilot if you are not sure that he has seen you. One final point — some paraglider pilots seem to feel that because their canopies are slow moving, faster craft such as hang gliders, sailplanes and so on should give way to them. While there is some truth in the suggestion that those craft have a greater speed to call upon, it is an EQUAL responsibility to avoid each other.

A busy day at Tailbridge — it is vital every pilot understands the anti-collision rules to be able to fly safely with others. (L. Addy)

Air law

One misconception that people entering the sport sometimes hold is that paragliding is not subject to air law. We are, however, sharing the airspace with a wide variety of other users and having laws and regulations helps to keep us, and them safe. Firstly we need to build up a mental picture of the way airspace is arranged. The air in the UK is divided into two broad chunks — that above 24,500ft and that below. The top chunk is known as the Upper Flight Information Region (UFIR). This is not particularly relevant to us. The lower chunk is sub-divided into the London and the Scottish FIRs. Within these areas there are a number of different types of controlled airspace we need to know about.

Airways

These are the roads of the air. They are (usually) ten nautical miles wide and have a lower and an upper level. These levels vary and for each one you need to consult an air chart. The levels are printed along each one like road numbers and may say (for example) FL75. This means that the base of this particular airway is at a Flight Level of 7,500 ft. A glider (that includes paragliders) is permitted to cross certain airways, though this is prohibited for many . However, it is rather like a hedgehog crossing the road. Therefore the rules are self-evident — keep a good look-out, cross quickly and in a straight line at 90°. For obvious reasons, you must be flying in full visual meteorological conditions, that is 8km visibility, clear of cloud by 1,500 metres horizontally and 1,000ft vertically. (Yes metres and feet are mixed!) Visual flight rules (VFR) are of course only applicable during the day. For the purposes of air law "day" is defined as from $1/2$ an hour before sunrise to $1/2$ an hour after sunset. Do not forget that if you are at altitude the sun will still be visible to you well after it is dark in the landing area.

Control areas

Control areas are found above aerodromes — they are the roundabouts of the sky where the airways meet. Very often, the airways descend in steps to the control area. Some are "crossable" and others are not. You will need to consult an up-to-date reference to find out which are which. Some of the control areas are known as control zones. As a general rule, a "zone" is airspace that extends from the ground upwards. An "area" is one that is from one given altitude to another. As always there are exceptions to this — Danger Areas, for example, (over military ranges etc) obviously start at ground level.

Control Traffic Areas (CTAs)

A control traffic area is an airspace in which there is air traffic control available.

Terminal manoeuvring areas (TMAs)

These are a sort of super roundabout found over major airports. Within them the air traffic is directed by the airport control tower. While it is possible to have radio contact if you have the right equipment and a suitable licence to use it, it is impractical for a paraglider to manoeuvre to order and the sheer volume of traffic around major airports make TMAs effectively out of bounds.

Air traffic zones (ATZs)

These comprise the restricted airspace belonging to smaller aerodromes. They start at ground level and go up to 2,000ft, within a radius of two nautical miles of the aerodrome. If the longest runway is longer than 1,850 metres the boundary is too close (less than one and a half nautical miles) and so the ATZ is increased to a radius of 2.5 nautical miles. There are a variety of grades of ATZ, ranging from prohibited, through those requiring prior or radio permission to penetrate. Your club can advise you of the situation locally.

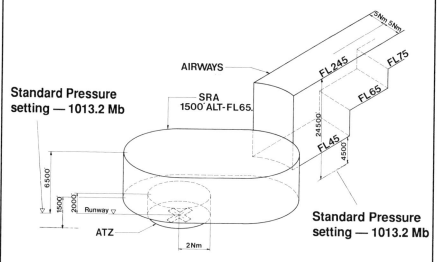

Fig 28. Aerodrome showing the air traffic zone. The special rules area and an airway 'stepping down' to meet it. The illustration shows only one airway stopping at the SRA boundary. In fact there may be more than one and they may well continue above, through and beyond the SRA.

Special rules zones (SRZs) and Special rules areas (SRAs)

There are a few SRAs and SRZs where gliders are permitted to enter under the same rules as those outlined under Airways. Local site guides will usually specify these. The vast majority, however, are prohibited airspace to us.

Military aerodrome traffic zones (MATZs)

As the name makes clear, these comprise the controlled airspace surrounding military air bases. They are made up of two parts — the inner Air Traffic Zone (ATZ), which is prohibited to us, and an outer zone in which you are permitted to penetrate. That is the law: however, it it would be extremely unwise to spend any length of time in an area where pilots who have a tremendous workload and are probably under training are very likely to be encountered. A MATZ typically has a radius of five nautical miles from the centre of the longest runway and extends to 3,000 ft above ground level. In addition, there is a stub *(see fig 29)* five nautical miles long and four wide, extending from 1,000ft up to 3,000 ft above ground level.

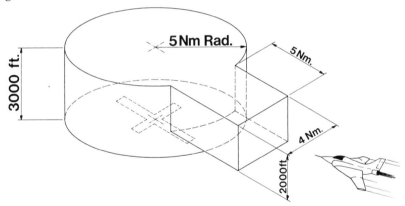

Fig 29. The dimensions of a typical military aerodrome traffic zone. (The ATZ is not shown). Note the 'stub' is in line with the longest runway.

Areas of intense aerial activity (AIAA)

This is a catch-all for any other area where there is a high risk of encountering other aircraft, such as an area used for aerobatics. Whilst not specifically prohibited to us, the same provisos apply as for a MATZ.

Airspace categories

There are six basic categories of airspace, but for our purposes we can break that down to three.

    1. Categories A,B,C, D. These are controlled airspace and effectively

Above: *Reserve deployment (Fred Stockwell)*

Right: *Sarah Fenwick flies her Voodoo above Reunion Island. (B. Goldsmith)*

prohibited to paragliders unless they are in radio contact with the air traffic controller. (There are a few exceptions which can be crossed in full VMC)

2: Category E (At present this consists of Scottish TMA below 6,000ft, Scottish CTR and Belfast TMA.) These areas are accessible to us in full VMC (5km visibility, 1,500m horizontally clear of cloud and 1,000ft vertically). 3.

3: Category F (advisory routes) and category G (the open FIR) have the same criteria above 3,000ft AMSL. (Above 10,000ft visibility must be 8km.) This comprises all the rest of the sky.

Below 3,000ft AMSL the rules are relaxed for aircraft moving at less than 140knots. VMC becomes: clear of cloud, and in sight of the ground with visibility of 1,500m. In other words you may circle to cloudbase if you are within this category but may not enter the cloud. However uncontrolled airspace is exactly that: uncontrolled, and civilian and military aircraft are free to make use of it just as we are. There is also the possibility that a Purple Airway may be notified at short notice. This is a Royal flight path and any penetration is not permitted.

Danger areas, Prohibited areas, Restricted areas

Dotted all over your airchart you will also find areas of prohibited or restricted airspace. These reflect ground-based activities such as sensitive military bases or ranges, nuclear power stations etc.

Danger areas are very often military ranges or some similar hazard. They can be active permanently or only at certain times. If you have certain prior knowledge that they are inactive they can be crossed (usually this means being in radio contact with ATC to request permission). Otherwise they are prohibited. Each danger area has a code, for example D 503/12. This means this is danger area 503 (In fact number 03 above 50° latitude) and extends to an altitude of 12,000ft.

High intensity radio transmission area

Airspace of defined dimensions within which there is radio energy of an intensity that may cause interference or even damage to radio and navigation equipment. Certain areas emit signals (microwaves, radar etc) that can be harmful to pilots.

Bird sanctuaries

Usually these are breeding colonies of rare birds. Unfortunately some, such as gannets, like to nest in areas of good ridge lift! Some are out of bounds in the breeding season, a few are prohibited at all times.

Sharing uncontrolled airspace

The major risk of collision in uncontrolled airspace is with other gliders (whether rigid, hang or para) as we all fly the same terrain and in the same way. *The anti-collision rules are reproduced in Chapter 24, under Site discipline — rules of the air.* The second group of air users that concerns us comprises military aircraft with crews under training. Their operations are often carried out at low level, high speed, and with their pilots doing their best to remain hidden by the terrain. They are concentrated in the more remote and hilly parts of the UK — exactly those areas most used by paragliders. Fortunately, the Royal Air Force usually operates on weekdays, except for major exercises which are usually well publicised through a NOTAM (notice to airmen). As a sport, paragliding is predominantly a weekend activity. However, there is still a very real possibility of conflict. A number of steps have been taken to minimise the risk of collision. Many of our major sites are marked on the air charts and some have a voluntarily agreed avoidance zone (again, your club guide will advise you). It is obvious that this is no protection if you are flying a minor site or have left the ridge on a cross-country flight. If this is likely to be the case, you should use the Civil Advance Notification Procedure (CANP) by dialling 0800515544 . You will be asked where you are planning to fly, the grid reference of the site, the nearest town, the time and area of intended activity and the scale of that activity. Given five hours notice, the information should appear on all pilots' bulletin boards. But even if you can not give that much notice it is still worth ringing. Note that the resultant CANP tells pilots of your presence so that they can be careful to keep a look out for you. It does not deny them the right to fly there. For details of royal flights, air displays or other short-term airspace restrictions, phone 0500 354802.

ALFENS (military Automated Low Flying Enquiry & Notification Service) is basically a computerised method of distributing CANP information and could be of benefit as it should speed up the time taken to relay information received on 0800 515544.

General flying rules

1. A glider shall not be operated in a negligent or careless manner so as to endanger life or property, nor be flown in such proximity to other aircraft as to create a danger of collision, nor in formation without the prior agreement of the pilots.

2. No person may be carried except in that part of the aircraft designed for the purpose, or be drunk in the aircraft.

3. Nothing shall be dropped from the aircraft other than a person by parachute in an emergency, articles for life-saving, or ballast in the form of fine dry sand or water.

4. A pilot, on meeting hazardous conditions in flight, shall as soon as possible report to the appropriate Air Traffic Control, information helpful to the safety of other aircraft.

5. A glider shall not fly over built-up areas below, either such height as will allow it to land clear or, 1,500 ft above the highest fixed object within 2,000ft of the aircraft, whichever is the higher. In any case, an aircraft may not be flown nearer than 500ft to any person, vehicle, vessel or structure, except when taking off, landing or hill-soaring.

There are a number of other rules that are designed for powered aircraft and are not directly relevant to paragliders. However, because they may help us understand the likely actions of other air users they are worth

Two canopies prepare to launch. (M. Aston)

Assisted Alpine launch. (Fred Stockwell)

knowing. The most useful of these are:

● When following a prominent ground feature (a motorway, railway or river for example) the aircraft shall keep the feature to its left.

● When not ridge soaring, an aircraft shall overtake on the right.

● The Quadrantal rule: Above 3,000ft AMSL aircraft will generally cruise at specific altitudes depending on their direction of track. Flying on a heading of between 0-89 degrees (ie between north & east) this will be at odd thousands of feet, (7,000, 9,000ft etc); 90-179 degrees (east to south) at odd thousands +500ft (eg 7,500ft); 180-269 degrees (south to west) even thousands of feet; 279-260 (west to north) even thousands plus 500.

Altimeters, air charts and radios

Knowing about the airspace is totally useless if you do not know where you are. Firstly, you must know your height, and for this you require an altimeter. This can be set to various references.

1. **QNH**. This means that zero on the altimeter is equal to sea-level.

2. **QFE**. This means zeroed to specific altitude, for example the take-off point or the anticipated landing field.

3. **Pressure Altitude.** This means set to a standard pressure setting (1,013.2mb). All the airspace above 3,000ft is based on this setting so this will tell you where you are relative to, say, an airway. As the pressure changes this means that airspace effectively moves up and down, so using air pressure as a datum prevents different aircraft having different readings when they are in fact at the same height.

Air charts

Air charts are the maps that contain all the information outlined above. While it is invaluable to become familiar with them, actually using them to navigate is extremely difficult. The practical solution is to copy the airspace relevant to your planned flight onto an ordinary Ordnance Survey, or similar, map to refer to in flight.

Radios

It is illegal to transmit from the air with other than an airband radio. To use the vast majority of airband frequencies you require a radio telephony licence. This is necessary if you wish to talk to a MATZ controller to get permission to penetrate his ATZ for example. There are, however, a few frequencies that are allocated to gliding and one of these (129.9mhz) is used (though not exclusively) by hang glider and paraglider pilots. You do not need to pass an exam to obtain a licence to use these gliding frequencies but you must maintain radio discipline and not use them to "chat". The frequencies currently available in the UK are:

129.900	*Mhz Volmet (forecast service);*	
129.975	North	126.600
130.100	South	128.600
130.125	Scottish	125.725
130.400	National	135.375

The emergency distress channel 121.500 is constantly monitored.

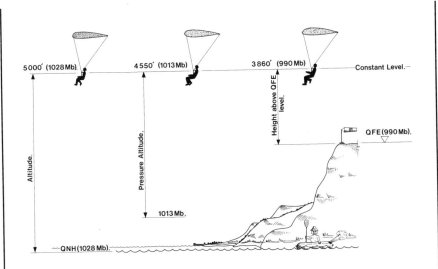

Fig 30: Altimeter settings

Meteorology

The weather is a colossal subject. In this section the intention is to introduce briefly some of the phenomena a paraglider pilot is likely to encounter or that are of particular interest to us.

Forecasts

Weather forecasts are available from a variety of sources. The most obvious is television. The BBC forecasts are excellent for establishing a visual picture of what is happening and, if you are familiar with the synoptic charts, you can glean a good deal of information that the presenter does not have time to spell out. Satellite photos are invaluable for assessing cloud cover. The downfall of these forecasts from our point of view is that they are very general and give no indication of the change of wind speed with height, and they rarely mention convection.

Radio forecasts fall into three categories. General "it will be a nice day" types are of little use to us. Specific forecasts, such as the maritime ones are good for approaching weather and surface winds (provided you know where "Dogger" or "Fastnet" actually are).

Volmet is a constant transmission of actual weather data of interest to air-users. It has a number of disadvantages, however. It tells you what is happening now rather than forecasting what is going to happen, and you may have to wait some time to hear the weather for your specific region. In many parts of the UK it is difficult or impossible to receive.

AERODROME INFORMATION

Aerodrome-Civil .... ⊗ or ○

Aerodrome-Civil, limited or no facilities .... ○

Heliport-Civil .... Ⓗ

Aerodrome-Government, available for Civil use. SEE UK AIP AGA 0-5 .... ◎

Aerodrome-Government .... ◎

Heliport-Government .... Ⓗ

Aerodrome-Disused or Abandoned. Shown for navigational
landmark purposes only. See AIC 46/91. .... ⊗ ⊗

AERODROME ELEVATION. Numerals adjacent to aerodrome indicate elevation
of aerodrome in feet above Mean Sea Level. 250 250

CUSTOMS AERODROMES are distinguished by a pecked line around
the name of the aerodrome. .... ⌐CAMBRIDGE¬

RUNWAY LENGTH. Active land aerodromes with a runway or landing strip,
regardless of surface, of 1850m or over, are indicated by a dot shown
within the aerodrome symbol. .... ⊙ ◎

Aerodrome Light Beacon .... ☆FIG : ⌐⌐ ˙ ☆FIR : ⌐⌐ ˙

Site of Intensive Microlight Flying .... Ⓜ
Intensive Microlight Activity also takes place at certain Licensed and Unlicensed
Aerodromes. See UK AIP RAC 5-1.

Glider Launching Site. UK AIP RAC 5-1. See Legend Note 8.
a. Primary activity at locations .... (cables) Ⓖ Ⓖ
b. Additional activity at locations .... (cables) ⊞ ⊞
Launch cables may be carried to 2000ft AGL.

Aerodrome Traffic Zone (ATZ). See Legend Note 1.
Regulated Airspace from the surface to 2000ft above the level of the
aerodrome within a circle centred on the notified mid-point of the
longest runway, radius 2·0NM (RW⩽1850m) or 2·5NM (RW>1850m)

Outside the notified hours of operation of an ATZ (as amended by NOTAM) pilots
should;
a. Endeavour to establish two-way R/T communication with the aerodrome.
b. Conduct their flight in the vicinity of the aerodrome in accordance with RULE 17,
   RULES OF THE AIR REGULATIONS 1991.

FOR CURRENT STATUS, AVAILABILITY, RESTRICTIONS AND WARNINGS APPLICABLE TO
AERODROMES SHOWN ON THIS CHART CONSULT AIR INFORMATION PUBLICATIONS AND
AERODROME OPERATORS OR OWNERS. PORTRAYAL DOES NOT IMPLY ANY RIGHT TO USE AN
UNLICENSED AERODROME WITHOUT PERMISSION.

MAGNETIC VARIATION
LINES OF EQUAL MAGNETIC VARIATION
(ISOGONALS) ARE SHOWN FOR JUNE 1992 ...... 6½°W
ANNUAL CHANGE 9' (decreasing)

Air chart symbols: The above are those that are found on UK 1:50,000
aircharts and which are particularly relevant to paraglider pilots.

HAZARD AND OTHER INFORMATION

FREE-FALL PARACHUTING SITE. UK AIP RAC 5-1.
Parachutists may be expected within the airspace contained
in a circle radius 1·5NM or 2NM of the DZ up to FL150. Night
parachuting may take place at any of the sites shown on this chart.

CABLE LAUNCH PARASCENDING PARACHUTE SITE. UK AIP RAC 5-1. See Legend Note 8.

a. Primary activity at locations . . . . (cables)
b. Additional activity at locations . . . . (cables)

> BAPC notified sites (with site elevations) where activity exceeds 500ft AGL are shown
> on this chart. Launch cables may be carried to 2000ft AGL.

HANG GLIDER LAUNCHING SITE. UK AIP RAC 5-1. See Legend Note 8.

a. Foot Launch Site . . . .

b. Cable Launch Site . . . . cables

> BHGA notified most commonly used Foot Launch Sites and those Cable Launch Sites
> (with site elevations) where activity exceeds 500ft AGL are shown on this chart.
> Launch cables may be carried to 2000ft AGL.

AIR NAVIGATION OBSTACLES

Exceptionally High Obstacle (Lighted)
1000ft or more AGL. Single, Multiple . . . . *1978*/(1031) *2297*/(1050)

Single Obstacle (Unlighted) . . . . *825*/(350)

Multiple Obstacle (Lighted) . . . . *1614*/(505)

Cable joining Obstacles . . . . cables

Numerals in italics indicate elevation of top of obstacle above Mean Sea Level. Numerals
in brackets indicate height of top of obstacle above local Ground Level. Obstacles
annotated 'flarestack' burn off high pressure gas. The flame, which may not be visible
in bright sunlight, can extend up to 600ft above the installation.

> LAND SITED OBSTACLES KNOWN TO THE AUTHORITY WHICH ATTAIN OR EXCEED A HEIGHT
> OF 300FT ABOVE LOCAL GROUND LEVEL ARE SHOWN ON THIS CHART. DUE ALLOWANCE
> FOR THESE CRITERIA MUST BE MADE WHEN DETERMINING SAFETY HEIGHT/ALTITUDE.
> EXCEPTIONALLY, A SMALL NUMBER OF OBSTACLES BELOW 300FT AGL ARE SHOWN FOR
> LANDMARK PURPOSES. PERMANENT OFF-SHORE OIL AND GAS INSTALLATIONS ARE SHOWN
> REGARDLESS OF HEIGHT CATEGORY. UK AIP RAC 5-1.

Marine Light . . . . ● Fl(3)30·0secs   Lightship . . . . . 🗼 FlWR12·0secs
(Normally shown if visibility range is not less than 15NM.)

MAXIMUM ELEVATION FIGURES (MEF)

3² Maximum Elevation Figures are shown in quadrangles
bounded by graticule lines for every half degree
of latitude and longitude. MEFs are represented
in thousands and hundreds of feet above mean
sea level. Each MEF is based on information available concerning
the highest known feature in each quadrangle, including terrain
and obstacles and allowing for unknown features.
NB THIS IS NOT A SAFETY HEIGHT

Telephone forecasts

Again there are the general type which are often available for a small region. This does make them more useful as local conditions, such as hill or coastal fog etc, may be mentioned. There is also a service in the UK known as Airmet. Airmet offers two services. One gives the weather for the following 24 hours, and one for the following 12 (i.e. that day). These are excellent as they give the most valuable information from our point of view — wind speeds at different heights. They also warn of turbulence, freezing levels and cloud types and coverage. The latter is expressed in octares (eighths). Airmet can also be subscribed to as a written forecast if you have a fax machine. A gliding supplement is available which gives information about wave or thermal activity, cloud types etc.

UK Airmet telephone numbers (1992)
These forecasts are updated each day at 0600hrs, 1200hrs and 1800hrs.
Southern Region 0891 500 693
Northern Region 0891 500 692
Scottish Region 0891 500 691
Planning information, Airmet forecasts for the following day.
Metplan Southern 0891 500 752
Metplan Northern 0891 500 751

As a general rule, pilots look out of the window first, then watch the TV. If the forecast is good — "a bright sunny day with light westerly winds" — they then set out. If it is poor — "gales and sleet" — they obviously do not bother. If the forecast implies it may be OK, then a call to Airmet may be advisable. If you are planning a cross-country flight then it is worthwhile obtaining the gliding supplement. This is the usual procedure for competition organisers etc who may even call their local airports to request the "actuals" (actual current weather). This is not a general service to sport flyers. The latest developments in forecasting involve hang gliding and paragliding clubs actually building their own weather stations, which they site in a suitable spot and which use a portable phone or are wired to a nearby line. Current technology allows the forecast data to be converted into a simulated voice that can be rung to give us our own "actual" data. (The publishers of this book have provided the necessary facilities for just such a service in the Yorkshire Dales.)

Fax forecasts

If you have a Group 3 fax machine it is also possible to obtain a fax forecast including synoptic charts and winds at altitude in the UK. With a suitable dish antenna and a personal computer you can even grab data and weather information direct from satellites, however the scale of the images means that it is not really very useful for forecasting for a small region.

Cloud types

Clouds are categorised according to their altitude and shape. There are three main categories.

Cirrus. These are the highest clouds, at 18,000 ft (5,500m) or more, they are composed of ice crystals.

Stratus. These are featureless layers of cloud.

Cumulus. Heaped piles of cloud caused by convection.

The latter two categories can be sub-divided again by height. The prefix "Alto" is added to identify clouds above 6,500ft (2,000m) and the prefix "cirro" to identify those at Cirrus levels. As a general rule, the high level clouds do not affect us directly, though they are a valuable indicator of what the weather is likely to do. The cloud types that directly concern us are, firstly, low stratus clouds. Are they going to cover the hills or cause visibility problems when airborne? A specific type of low stratus is orographic cloud. This is a blanket of cloud that clings to the surface, usually on the windward face of a hill. It is worth pointing out that these clouds can form quite quickly and if you are already airborne and notice wisps forming over the surface of the hill, you should land immediately.

The second type of cloud we are concerned with is cumulus cloud. Cumulus clouds are formed by the condensation of water vapour in rising air (convection) and therefore indicate areas of lift. Where there is lift there is also turbulence, so they also signal caution for the inexperienced pilot.

Cumulus clouds vary from the tiny "balls of cotton wool" that have little or no effect on us, through weak, medium and strong thermal clouds right up to the dark-bottomed cumulo-nimbus clouds which mark violent updraughts and severe turbulence. *Cumulus clouds are mentioned again under "thermals" and in Chapter 27, Cross-country flight.*

Another cloud type that directly concerns us is a type of alto-stratus known as a lenticular. Lenticular clouds are easily identified as they are smooth and lens-shaped and they do not move across the sky with the wind. They are usually arranged in "stacks" or as a series of "bars" at 90° to the wind direction. These clouds mark the presence of atmospheric wave, which is an important source of lift and turbulence *(see "wave", below and in Chapter 27)*.

Depressions, fronts, and high pressure systems

The dynamics of weather systems make up an interesting but complex subject which is well explained in several books. Very briefly, the sun heats the earth more at the equator (where its rays pass through the atmosphere at almost 90° to the earth's surface) and less at the poles. This sets up a circulation as air rises, moves horizontally and then sinks and flows back again. In some parts of the world this gives rise to regular and settled weather patterns. In those areas sandwiched between "competing" polar and equatorial systems, the weather is changeable and much more difficult to predict. The UK and most of North America fall into this

Ready for tow launch. (Sky Systems)

category. We can, however, read the weather as it approaches if we have some understanding of the main features.

Depressions and fronts

These are areas of relatively low atmospheric pressure. Air can rise easily in these regions and, as a result, depressions are frequently associated with cloud and rain. Depressions often form where air masses of different temperatures meet. The division between these air masses is known as a front. Because of the different characteristics of the air mass on each side, these fronts may develop "waves" along their length. The actual process is triggered by the Jetstream and is beyond the scope of this book. A wave on a front is the first sign of a depression being created (*fig 29*). As the depression develops, the pressure drops and the winds increase (*fig 32*). The air masses are now arranged in sectors and are divided by a warm front followed by a cold front. As the depression gradually fills and weakens the cold front overtakes the warm front and the result is an occluded front. To clarify the different characteristics (*figs 33, 34 & 35*) show a cross-section through each type of front.

As a warm front approaches, cirrus cloud appears and this cloud gradually lowers and thickens into nimbo-stratus or strato-cumulus, the wind "backs" — that is swings anti-clockwise, and strengthens. As the front passes the rain slackens, cloudbase rises and the wind "veers" (swings clockwise, from south west to west for example). A cold front is marked by heavy rain and perhaps thunder with cumulo-nimbus clouds if the front is an active one. There may be "gust front" extending well ahead of cu-nimb clouds making flying in their vicinity very dangerous. As the front arrives the wind increases and veers. After the passage of a cold front the cloudbase rises again and the cold air may give a sharp temperature gradient, this leads to active convection and the formation of cumulus clouds.

Paraglider pilots do not need to understand how the weather develops in order to fly, but the more we understand the easier it is to make accurate predictions of what is coming next. This obviously offers benefits both in safety and in saving wasted journeys. Take the potential cross-country pilot: by studying a synoptic chart (one showing depressions and fronts, using isobars, and broad lines to show fronts), the pilot can see that there is a cold front expected to pass quickly overhead on Friday. This means that, by Saturday afternoon, he can expect a good temperature gradient (temperature falling rapidly with altitude gain) in the cold sector and therefore there are likely to be strong convection currents (thermals). This means good weather for altitude and distance flying.

A pilot noticing cirrus clouds building in the west, sometimes noticeable as a "halo" around the sun, can deduce that a warm front is approaching and the weather will soon deteriorate. Fronts are shown as lines on a weather map. These lines indicate the position of the front on the

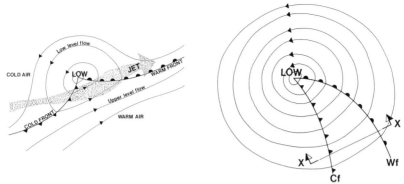

Fig 31. Formation of a low pressure system

Fig 32. Plan of low pressure system showing fronts

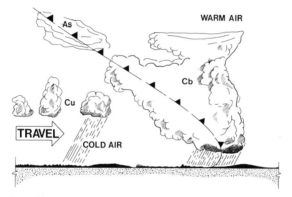

Fig 33. Arctic cold front showing clouds. Cu = Cumulus; As = Alto Stratus; Cb = cumulonimbus.

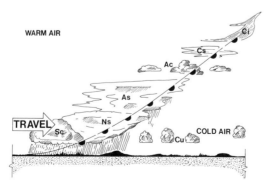

Fig 34. Warm front showing clouds. Ci =Cirrus; Cs = Cirro-stratus; Ac = Alto cumulus; As = Alto stratus; Ns = Nimbo-stratus; Sc = Strato-cumulus; Cu = Cumulus.

Cloudbase over Brighton. (Sky Systems)

Busy launch site, California. (Fred Stockwell)

Foot launch in the snow, Zermatt, Switzerland. (L. Addy)

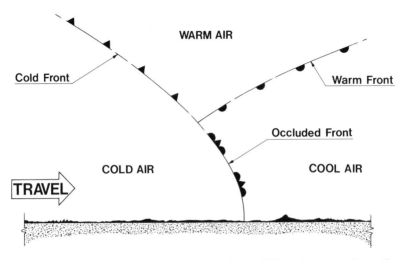

Fig 35. An occluded front. The faster moving cold front has caught up the warm front and is squeezing it upwards, the depression is now filling and weakening.

ground. In reality, the gradient of a front is around 1° or 2° and so a frontal zone can easily be 150 miles wide. The illustrations have an exaggerated vertical scale so that they will fit on the page!

Remember Buy's Ballots Law — this is a simple rule to help you remember your position relative to a depression. In the northern hemisphere, if you stand with your back to the wind, the centre of the low will be on your left.

High pressure systems

These are the opposite of depressions. Because the pressure is high, there is little rising air. The sky is often cloudless and there is little wind. If the pressure remains high for some time, dust and dirt in the atmosphere may not be circulated and so the air at low level (often trapped beneath a temperature "inversion", see below) becomes hazy and visibility diminishes. If there is sufficient wind to fly, the conditions are often very smooth, but the lack of any convection means that cross-country flying is virtually impossible as all the air is gradually sinking. The airflow around a high pressure system is in a clockwise direction in the northern hemisphere.

Thermals

The radiation given out by the sun covers a wide spectrum of wavelengths. The heat radiation, however, has very little effect on the atmosphere (unless it happens to be very wet or dirty) and most of it is reflected or reaches the ground. Some surfaces, such as water or green grass, reflect much of the heat and are slow to warm up. Other surfaces, such as dry sand, Tarmac or rocks, absorb heat and may warm quite quickly. This difference in warming is also compounded by uneven ground or aspect (a south facing slope is warmer than a north face, a west face is warmer in the evening) and other factors. A result of this differential warming is that the hot surfaces then warm the air around and above them. Like most other substances, when air is heated its molecules become excited and bounce around more vigorously. The warm air expands and, in doing so, it becomes less dense. If the sun is still shining and the warming process continues, the "bubble" of warm air will grow larger and larger and become lighter and lighter. Eventually it will break away from the surface and float up through the denser and cooler air around it, gradually cooling as it goes. Eventually it reaches a level where the surrounding air is at a similar temperature and pressure and there it stops.

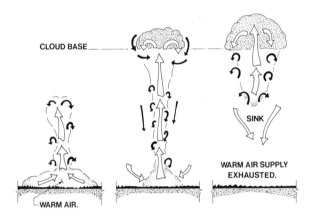

Fig 36. The birth and growth of a thermal to form a cumulus cloud.

The warm air very often contains more moisture than the surrounding cooler air and as the thermal rises it may reach the condensation level (dew-point), and a cloud is formed. The condensation level occurs when the parcel of air is cooled to the point of saturation and the moisture it contains condenses as cloud — air holds less moisture at lower temperatures. The process of condensation is a heat-producing reaction and so the thermal receives a final boost which is why cumulus clouds are heaped up and not just flat. A thermal may be stopped at a low altitude if there is a layer of warmer air. These layers are known as inversions (because they are inverse to the usual gradient of temperature reducing with height). Very often the temperature does not reduce uniformly as you climb and so the thermal may be rising strongly then slow down or vice-versa as it passes through these layers. It is possible to plot the progress of a thermal if you know the temperature gradient. Fig 37 shows a temperature trace for a

Sunset over the sea. (Fred Stockwell)

particular day. As you can see, it generally becomes cooler as you gain altitude. This cooling is known as the lapse rate, and various factors affect this rate.

Dry air (that is containing no cloud or mist) has a specific rate of cooling with altitude. This is known as the Dry Adiabatic Lapse Rate (DALR). The DALR is approximately a cooling of 1 °C with every 100 metres of altitude (even more roughly 3°C with every 1,000 feet). Armed with this knowledge, a thermometer and an altimeter you can predict the climb rate of thermals and the height of the cloudbase.

Pressure also decreases with height, on most weather forecasts the pressure is shown in millibars (mb) or hectopascals (hPa). Both units have identical values and are interchangeable. For our purposes we can assume pressure drops by one millibar every 30ft or 9.8 metres. In fact it is slightly less than that at sea level and slightly more at 5,000ft.

There is also a Saturated Adiabatic Lapse Rate (SALR) which is approximately half the dry rate, at 0.5°C per 100 metres (or 1.5°C per 1,000 feet). The saturated lapse rate is the cooling rate of air saturated with condensing water droplets, that is cloud. In practice, the lapse rates vary enormously due to all kinds of outside factors, and the solid line on the illustration shows a temperature trace that is realistic for an "unstable" day with some useful thermals. The broken line shows two other features that may occur.

The first is an isothermal layer. This is simply a layer of air that does not change temperature. The second is an inversion, a layer of air that actually increases in temperature with height. This generally occurs in a region of high pressure — the air has been descending and this process compresses and warms the airmass. Thermals will of course be slowed or stopped by such features (depending on the strength and temperature of the thermal relative to the warm layer). This explains why a thermal can suddenly stop or can climb in bursts, or why only one or two thermals from particularly hot sources can penetrate to form clouds. The inversion may be quite high, so thermals can still be felt even though they never reach high enough to form clouds. Because the dry and saturated lapse rates are linked, you can determine the strength of a thermal from its vertical development. Towering cumulus clouds mean powerful lift, wispy ones (unless just forming) mean weaker lift.

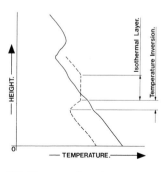

Fig. 37. Temperature trace

Wave

Wave (or lee wave) is a phenomenon caused when the wind is blowing over a series of hills. As we have seen in the section on ridge soaring, the air is accelerated as it is squeezed over the brow of a hill. This process adds energy to the flow. If the hill is solitary then that energy is dissipated as airflow downwind of the hill gradually flattens out again into a horizontal flow. If there is a line of hills the energy has no time to dissipate before it is being reinforced by another injection of faster, vertically moving air. The result of this happening several times is that each fresh input pushes the wave of lifting air higher than the last. If there is a layer of stable air above the hills, the process is strengthened as it sinks back quickly after being pushed up by the rising air. The oscillation can then build up a powerful system. It is not unusual for a line of hills perhaps only a few hundred feet high to set up wave lift extending to 10,000 or 20,000 feet. When the moist low level air is pushed up to these heights the moisture condenses and clouds are formed. These lenticular clouds are arranged along the crest of the wave of air and so are at 90° to the wind direction. Because they are being formed at the front by rising air but then dissipating as the air descends again, they remain stationary.

The crest of the wave will occur some way downwind of the hill that is causing it, hence the term "lee wave". At the bottom of the wave the wind — which may have a considerable velocity — may have to make a sudden change in direction. The result is the same as when there is an obstruction on the ground — the air "tumbles" and forms a rotor. This can result in very severe turbulence. As the windspeed changes, the wave position can move very quickly and may suddenly disappear altogether as the hills become "out of phase" for that strength. A spot that was enjoying good lift can be transformed fairly quickly into one that has descending air or even rotor. Wave may be identified by the changes of windspeed on the ground. It is not unusual to pass trees blowing in a good wind and a few miles further on to see smoke drifting slowly. If you are on a hill and the wind is light but it seems to be strong at altitude or nearby, exercise caution as it is likely you are in a localised "out of phase" sector. Once you are actually flying within the rising wave, the lift tends to be very smooth indeed and the greatest heights achieved by hang gliders and paragliders in the UK have been in this form of lift. Fig 38 shows the ideal conditions for lee wave production. Increasing wind strength with height. An unstable layer with a stable layer just above the top of the ridge capped by more unstable air (see temperature trace at left hand side of diagram).

Sea-breeze fronts

One other phenomenon that can give excellent flying conditions is a sea-breeze front. On hot, light-wind, days the land is much warmer than the sea. As the warmer air over the land gradually reduces in density and pressure, the cooler air from the sea pushes in below it to form an on-shore

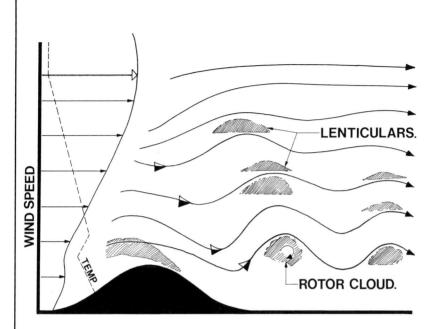

Fig 38. Cross section showing formation of lee-wave

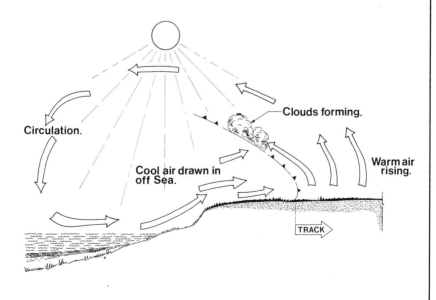

Fig 39. Formation of a sea breeze front

breeze. These breezes may be soarable on coastal sites. But the interesting thing is when this onshore breeze contacts a basically offshore wind.

The conflict between these air masses is resolved exactly like a weather front, with the lighter warm air flowing up over the wedge of cool dense air. If the coastline is steep or the gradient of the incoming maritime air is sufficient, an invisible ridge is formed which can create sufficient lift to be soarable. Where there is no significant obstacle on the ground, the sea breeze front can penetrate many miles inland. *See fig 39.*

Cross-country flight

To soar over the open countryside, having to navigate and find lift as you go, is one of the greatest challenges and most memorable experiences of paragliding. It is scarcely believable that pilots have crossed mountain ranges and deserts, and attained altitudes of thousands of metres, using an aircraft that they can carry in a rucksack. And having once experienced it, pilots always fly in the hope of being able to go even further next time. Cross-country flights can be achieved using any of the lift sources detailed previously in this book but typically rely on thermals. The potential XC pilot must first be able to recognise, and be prepared for, the right day.

Preparation

First check the forecast. If it is possible that you may fly a long way you may need to arrange how to get back home afterwards. Plan your likely route. At the current level of performance, pilots flying on a day with any significant wind will be obliged to travel in a predominantly down-wind direction. You will need a suitable map on which any airspace or other hazards should be accurately marked. Check your variometer and altimeter (there is nothing worse than the batteries dying just as you have left the hill behind you). Make sure you are properly clothed. It is far colder at altitude than on the ground. Assuming a standard dry adiabatic lapse rate, the temperature will drop about 3°C with every 1,000 feet. If the day does prove to have good thermals, you should try to choose the best time of day to leave the hill. If it is very hot and thermals are growing quickly, it is best to get away early as the growing cloud cover may overdevelop and result in either cumulo-nimbus clouds or in so much ground shadow that thermals cease to be produced. For this reason most of the best cross-country days are in spring and autumn when the air is relatively cold and the thermal cycle can last for much longer than in mid-summer. On the other hand, if the thermals are far apart, or if the sky downwind is too blue, your chances of a reasonable distance are reduced. However, as the cloudbase usually lifts during the day, the radius which you can search for new lift does increase.

A world record in the making! This photo is by Pierre Boullioux of Sup'Air taken en route to a new triangle world record in the French Alps.

When actually circling in a thermal, try to centre on the "core" — the lift may be only temporary and the thermal will be going up faster than you are, so it is quite easy to get left behind! Do not change the direction of your circling, but open out the pattern as the lift weakens and tighten as it strengthens. You may find that it is possible to fly at a slightly slower speed than usual if the lift is strong but be prepared to compensate quickly should you fly out of the lift. Once at cloudbase there is a definite temptation to go speeding off and explore. At a good altitude your groundspeed seems negligible and many pilots compensate by speeding up. The golden rule with an aircraft as slow and as inefficient as a paraglider is never leave lift. To fly cross-country in any but no-wind conditions or in certain timed competitions, the trick is to stay off the ground for as long as possible. Allow the drift of the wind to provide your distance for you. Another reason never to leave lift is that it is very often surrounded by sinking air, and you could lose altitude faster than you have gained it. After circling for a few miles your cloud finally ceases to lift. Look around for an active cloud to fly towards. With luck, the sink will only be gentle at this stage and your glide performance will take you to the next thermal where you can climb again. If no clouds are obviously waiting for you, study the ground. Is there an area that has been in sunshine for a while? Is there a likely thermal trigger point (a quarry or small town, or perhaps a windward ridge).

Always try to be aware of the position of the sun — the sheltered lee side of a hill that is angled into the sun, for instance, is a better bet than an area where the suns's rays are striking at a shallow angle. Needless to say, if you see a real give-away — such as circling birds or other gliders — that is where to go. It is worth mentioning at this point that on your first XC flights it is far easier if you do not go alone, another paraglider, hang glider or even a sailplane will give a wealth of information about the whereabouts of lifting or sinking air.

If you should elect to go crosswind to a thermal or likely spot, your ground speed will naturally drop. However, it does not make any difference to your performance through the air. It is air distance that is important. If there are no clues as to where to go next, then fly straight downwind. In this way your chances are as good as in any other direction and you will be covering ground at a better pace.

If the lift is strong, look up. If the cloud is large and solid looking, or if those around you have a good vertical development it is always worth flying in a straight line for a while to determine the edge of the lift: you may wish to fly on the edge of the thermal so that you can "escape" if the lift becomes too severe. Do not allow yourself to be sucked into cloud. Apart from the possibility of turbulence in powerful clouds they are also very wet, which will not do your canopy's performance any good. You will become disorientated in a matter of seconds and the chances of a mid-air collision increase dramatically. If you are very lucky you may find one of those clouds where it is possible to circle up the side without going right into it. Climbing above cloud on a glider is a rare and amazing experience. Do not forget that you are in uncontrolled airspace — or you certainly should be — and there may well be other traffic around. The visual flight rules are see and avoid. Do not let your eyes become glued to the variometer.

Flying with others

You already know about circling in the same direction as the other pilots in a thermal. It is equally important to give those below you plenty of room as they can not see you very well. If you wish to take any action, such as flying away from the thermal core and coming back, make sure that you do it in such a way that the others can see you and do not have to disrupt their patterns. Never tuck in directly behind another pilot: he can not see you very well and you will be flying in his vortices which will reduce your control. Always try to remain on the opposite side of the thermal from someone at the same altitude. If you have a good pattern established you may get the illusion that you are remaining stationary while he whizzes round you in huge circles — don't worry, it looks just the same to him.

Landing

Never, ever fly cross-country over terrain where you are not always within range of a suitable landing field. You may get away with it once or even twice, but you can bet that eventually you will end up in a tree/

water/ gorge etc. A height of 3,000ft will give you a search radius of about two miles for a suitable field. This area will be displaced downwind of course. You require a large flat field, if possible, with no stock or crops and without any power-lines — these are difficult to see from the air, so check for poles or pylons. Check the wind direction — there may be smoke or similar indicators but it can be surprisingly difficult to judge. The best way is to get a rough idea by watching your drift, or the drift of cloud shadows, and fine tuning as you make your approach. After landing, try to make a point of thanking the farmer and you may even be offered a cup of tea and the use of a phone. If it is a sparsely populated area, try to land near a road. If landing near a village do a quick aerial survey as you lose height to see if there is a phone box. Now all you have to do is get back home...

Out-and-return flights

In the sailplane world, defined XC flights have been the norm for several years. They generally take the form of an out-and-return or triangle flight. The benefits of a long flight where you end up back at launch are obvious, and as distances steadily increase hang gliders too are using this option in more and more instances. As yet paragliders are unable to make any significant progress into wind and so defined XC flights are confined to flights across wind and return, or those undertaken in nil-wind conditions (usually from a winch or Alpine launch). Turn points are generally recorded with a photograph. The progress of our sport has always mirrored that of hang gliding, and defined XC flight is sure to become one of the major areas of progress in the future.

Navigation

When flying cross-country it is vital to know where you are. Flying with a map is a necessity and on long flights to a specific goal, or in unfamiliar terrain, you may need to navigate using compass bearings. Navigation falls into two categories: planning and map reading.

Planning is done before take off and will consist of drawing your intended track on a map, ensuring you have marked and planned for any hazards, and worked out any compass bearings you may require. A very useful exercise is to mark a point perhaps 20 per cent of the distance to your goal, or 10km from the start, and time yourself to this point. In this way you can easily calculate your groundspeed and therefore your remaining time, or your likely distance in a certain time.

Compass bearings are complicated by the fact that the compass will point to magnetic north whereas the grid squares on your map will refer to true north. The difference is known as VARIATION. If you look at the map key it will tell you the amount of variation when that particular map was printed. (Yes it does change with time!)

Map reading in the air is vital to paraglider pilots. Unlike a powered aircraft we cannot simply stick to our intended track, we tend to go where the lift takes us. If you have done the groundspeed exercise then one hour into your flight you should know how far you are from launch and, together with your compass reading and ground features, should be able to plot your position. Needless to say if you are flying over desert or mountains then your compass bearings need to be accurate and up-to date. Some years ago a well known American hang glider pilot scored a zero flying in an Alpine competition for landing in the wrong country!

28 Plotting performance: the polar curve

When we talk of the performance of a paraglider, it is sometimes difficult to visualise how to obtain the best from it it various situations. It is possible to gather various pieces of information from tests that confirm that this model sinks at a rate of 1.7 metres per second at 17mph and so on. When we have sufficient data we can plot them on a graph and the result is a performance "map" of the craft. This graph is known as a polar diagram (*fig 40*). The polar curve of a craft is time-consuming and painstaking to produce, but once drawn it allows us to predict the paraglider's performance and so helps both designers and pilots. If we wish to know our sink-rate at 15mph we can simply read off the figure where the sink-rate axis corresponds to 15mph. Our best sink-rate is at the highest point on the graph and our best glide ratio in nil wind is at the point where a straight line drawn from 0mph on the axis just touches the curve (*fig 40*). We can also discover our performance in different situations. For example, if our canopy glides at 5:1 at 16mph but we have a headwind of 10mph, how fast should we fly to achieve our best gliding performance? We can plot this by drawing another straight line which just touches the curve but is drawn from the 10mph point on the horizontal speed axis (*fig 40*). You can now apply the same technique to asses the performance of the craft in any combination of lifting or sinking air, headwind or tailwind.

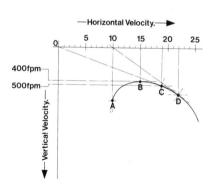

Fig 40. Polar curve —
A = point of stall at 10mph;
B = minimum sink 400 fpm at 15 mph;
C = maximum glide at 19 mph with 500 fpm sink;
D=best speed to fly with a 10mph headwind=22mph.

Canopy instability and recovery   **29**

A paraglider is virtually unique among aircraft in that it relies upon the weight of the pilot to maintain its shape and therefore the structural integrity of the wing. If the weight is reduced or removed or distributed wrongly, the wing may collapse. In addition, the aerofoil shape is maintained by internal air pressure. If this pressure is reduced or lost the wing is once again prone to distortion and collapse. This is addition to the usual unstable behaviour of any aerofoil when stalled. It is therefore vital that the pilot understands his craft's behaviour and is able to help prevent, or anticipate, any problems. The pilot must also be capable of recovering promptly should he find himself in an unstable situation.

Dealing with turbulence

Prevention is better than cure. Before discussing how to recover from unstable situations, it is worth trying to understand how they can occur and how to prevent them. Gusts, thermals and turbulent air are invisible, the only way you have of detecting them (apart from basic site and weather assessment of course) is by feel. Flying in rough air is all about feeling the canopy and reacting very quickly to the feedback it is giving you. The first rule is to maintain some pressure on the controls all the time in rough air. This gives you the option to speed up or slow down and also seems to pressurise the canopy to some extent, helping minimise wing tip tucks etc.

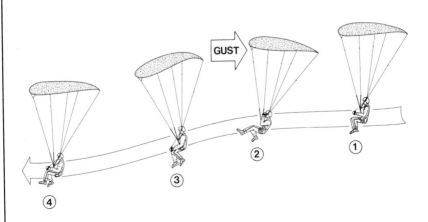

Fig 41: Flying in gusty conditions. 1. Flying around mid-brake position. 2. Encounters gust — canopy pitches back — brakes high to provide speed. 3. Flying into lull behind gust — canopy pitches forward — brakes applied to slow canopy down.. 4. Return to normal level flight.

The second rule is to try to keep the canopy directly above your head! (Fig 41) The commonest situation is that the wing suddenly surges forward over your head. The reason could be a gust from behind or a lull in the air in front of you, but your reaction must be to apply instantly the correct amount of brake to arrest the surge. A head-on gust or thermal will try to push the canopy back. React to this by adding speed, (Fig 41) but be careful — where there is a gust there is usually a lull behind it, and you do not want to hit that at full speed just as gravity is swinging you back under the canopy, so be ready to brake again the moment the canopy starts coming back.

Thirdly, maintain your course, do not allow turbulence (or a tuck) turn you without countering it with opposite brake.

You may find that you lose pressure on just one control: take a look to see if it is just soft or has tucked. If thermal or gust has just begun to deflate it brake until you feel contact with the wing again and at the same time balance the motion with a similar amount of brake on the other side. If it has collapsed then use the other brake to hold course while you pump it out *(see Asymmetric tuck).* If you begin to lose pressure on both controls when braking deeply let up smoothly, you may be approaching the stall.

If the canopy surges upwards and forwards then you have encountered a thermal. If it surges upwards and backwards then it is probably a gust. If you do not feel in control of the situation do not hesitate to land and fly again another day — don't forget you are doing this for fun!

CAUTION — WHILE IT IS DESIRABLE TO BE PRACTISED AND COMPETENT AT RECOVERY FROM STALLS, SPINS AND TUCKS, IT IS RECOMMENDED THAT BEFORE UNDERTAKING ANY OF THESE MANOEUVRES YOU RECEIVE ON-SITE BRIEFING FROM AN EXPERIENCED PILOT OR INSTRUCTOR . PRACTISE THEM OVER WATER, CARRY A RESERVE PARACHUTE SYSTEM AND ALLOW A 100 PER CENT MARGIN FOR ERROR WHEN ESTIMATING THE HEIGHT AND SPACE REQUIRED FOR RECOVERY.

Asymmetric tuck

This is perhaps the commonest situation. One end of the canopy collapses while the other part is still flying.

Recovery: If the canopy is turning towards the collapsed side and there is a danger of collision with the hill or with another pilot, carefully apply some opposite control to arrest or slow the turn. Give a long firm pull on the control on the collapsed side and it will re-inflate. This forces air forwards and opens the cell entries to the airflow. If the collapsed area is 60 per cent or more of the wing, treat as a front tuck (pump both sides). In this case, the controls on the collapsed side may have little air to move and the pumping action forces air through the internal vents.

Full front tuck

This occurs when the load on the front lines is substantially reduced — if the canopy overflies the pilot, for example, or in turbulence. The front "rolls" underneath. Recovery: Give a long firm pull on the controls; the canopy will re-inflate. This forces air in the canopy forwards and unrolls it.

Full (dynamic) stall

This occurs when the canopy loses virtually all forward airspeed and consequently internal pressure. It can only be induced by "flaring", that is by applying full brake on both sides, or by very severe turbulence. The canopy produces no lift but a large amount of drag and it falls behind the pilot, usually in a "horseshoe" shape.

Recovery: Firstly wait — you are much heavier than the canopy and you will swing back to a relatively normal position below it. If you have induced the stall, keep the controls depressed. If you let up too soon, the sudden reduction of drag just as the canopy is swinging forwards anyway may cause the canopy to dive down in front of you and tuck. Once stabilised smoothly, let up the controls to about 25 per cent. Be prepared to brake a little more if the canopy tries to overfly you. Do not let up suddenly or all the way.

Caution: some canopies "dislike" being in the horseshoe mode and thrash about above you, so care must be taken as they may recover unevenly and enter a spin.

Deep (parachutal) stall

A number of canopies can be stabilised in a deep stall. This is the state in which the canopy has little forward motion and the airflow over it is predominantly turbulent, creating no lift. However, the wing retains its shape and does not collapse. Its sink rate is very fast and normal control inputs are ineffective as there is little airflow over the controls. Some canopies can be deep stalled through gradually increasing braking. Others can only reach this state through the rear risers being pulled down.

Recovery: Some models can be recovered by vigorously depressing one control line, the canopy enters a turn, gaining airspeed and resumes normal flight. The other recovery technique is to flare hard with both controls and induce a full stall that can be recovered in the normal way.

Spins

A spin is an unstable state where half the wing is stalled and half is flying. This causes the canopy to rotate violently, often on its own axis. There is a risk of the canopy collapsing (half of it may be flying backwards) and it is possible for the lines to become twisted between the canopy and the pilot. A spin is induced when the paraglider is flown at a high angle of attack (ie with deep brake) and then the controls are simultaneously raised on one side and depressed on the other.

Recovery: Let up both controls to gain speed. As the wing regains flying speed, steer out of the turn. Caution: it is possible to achieve considerable airspeed in a spin and on recovery you must be prepared to damp out any tendency for the canopy to surge forwards as this can result in a tuck.

Other manoeuvres

360° turns

This is simply flying round in a circle. 360s are worth noting because they involve flying on a downwind leg (if there is any wind). Therefore, some planning is required — how far downwind will the drift be etc. A 360 is particularly useful for approaching some landing areas, and for thermalling where you can drift at the same speed as the thermal and so stay with it as it moves.

Spiral dives

A spiral dive is simply a series of tight 360° turns. It is very inefficient and so the canopy can lose height very rapidly — very useful for getting down quickly or combating strong lift. A spiral dive is induced by fully depressing one control and raising the other, gradually steepening the turn until the pilot is swung out from the canopy which can eventually be almost at 90° to the ground.

Caution: When recovering from a spiral dive you may have excessive airspeed. The canopy must be "damped" if it converts this energy into a climb, or you may either stall at the top of the climb-out or the canopy may tuck as the load on the front risers is momentarily reduced.

"Big ears"

This is the common name given to the practice of deliberately collapsing the cells at the tips. This has the effect of reducing the flying surface and so increasing the sink rate. It can be very useful indeed for combating strong lift (unlike a spiral dive, it can be done at low altitudes and without involving drifting downwind). Modern canopies are 'big eared' by grasping the outermost one or two A lines on each side, and pulling them out and down to induce the outermost cells to tuck.

A canopy must have A lines that go to the leading edge only to be capable of big-earing — this generally means three or more risers. Be careful of long risers — it is easy to pull the whole thing when trying to affect just a couple of lines andthereby inducing a front tuck.

If using this facility for the first time on a canopy always pull slowly and smoothly or, if possible, close one side at a time. To re-inflate the tip cells simply pump the controls as you would for a minor tuck.

"B" line stall

Some canopies can also be made to sink very quickly in a stable state by pulling down the centre lines and "breaking the back" of the canopy. This disrupts the airflow and destroys the aerofoil. The canopy must have three risers to make it possible to pull down only the centre lines.

"B" lining is a useful manoeuvre to lose height quickly. However, there are some potential problems. Some canopies will remain deep stalled, particularly if the pilot lets up very slowly. During a B line stall all the weight is through as little as eight lines which can put teriffic strain on the lines and attachment points. Know your canopy: always release smoothly but quickly and in the case of being "stuck" use deep brake then let up to allow the wing to surge forward. This will re-establish a correct airflow and the canopy will recover. If you pull very hard on the B lines the tips may come forward forming a horseshoe shape and descent will be very rapid. Before attempting this check the canopy's suitability with your instructor, dealer or manufacturer.

Front centre line stall.

Like the B-line stall, this breaks the back of the canopy, but fore and aft rather than across the span. The same provisos apply.

Emergency procedures
30

These fall into two distinct categories — equipment failure, and "sticky situations". Both can almost invariably be prevented by pre-flight checks and good flight-planning. The piece of equipment most likely to let a pilot down is between his ears!

Equipment failure

Broken or lost control line. A limited form of steering is available by adding pressure to the rear riser. Many canopies can be well controlled by weight shift. As it is difficult to flare with rear risers alone you should be prepared for a fast landing which may mean running or a PLF.

Other damaged lines. Generally, a paraglider will fly quite well with only a couple of lines missing (though it may have a tendency to turn). Land as soon as possible and have them replaced. If a lot are broken, after a mid-air collision for example, throw your reserve.

Major damage to the canopy harness or connections. If you have any control it is better to fly down as best you can. The only other option is to throw your reserve which of course can neither be steered nor flared.

Canopy inextricably twisted or tangled due to spin, severe turbulence or mid-air collision. Deploy your reserve, subject to the provisos above.

Deploying a reserve. If you do have to deploy the reserve during a spin, always try to throw it in the direction of the spin as it is less likely to get twisted up. As it opens, the main canopy may dive down in front of you. If so, it is a good plan to grab a piece of the leading edge. This will prevent it interfering with the reserve. If you have time you may be able to collapse the main canopy by pulling the tip lines until the canopy can be grabbed. Alternatively, pull in the centre A lines until the canopy can be held. When approaching the ground assume the position for a PLF.

Sticky situations

Being blown back over a hill. First check that any trim devices are fully off and that the controls are at maximum speed (against the keepers). If your canopy has the facility to close the ears, now is the time to use it. Your forward speed will increase slightly and your descent rate markedly. If these ploys do not work you are committed to top land. Look back over your shoulder. Can you land safely in the area where you will end up? If so, wait until touch-down then turn and run after the canopy collapsing it as you go. If the area looks unsuitable, try to track to the most suitable spot within range. Flying right off the end of the ridge may be an option. If the area behind you is really diabolical, such as a cliff-top or a spine backed ridge, and you have any significant height, continue to soar the ridge at minimum sink speed trying to gain as much height as possible. You may find that the lift extends to well behind the crest. When you are as high and as far back as possible turn downwind and make a run for it, retaining a little brake and being prepared for turbulence as you fly through any rotor. Note: if you have any control as you approach the ground, try to establish the wind direction. If you are in rotor it may be from any direction. Be prepared to PLF.

Remember that the above situation need never occur if you asses conditions properly, treat ridges with poor top-landing areas with respect and leave a greater margin for error.. Be aware of changing weather. If penetration does seem to be reducing, land quickly or at least track to one end of the ridge where flying out of the lift is possible if required.

Water landings. Once again, the emphasis here is on prevention through good flight planning rather than cure. However, if you should find yourself in a situation where a water landing is inevitable, try to prepare before you touch down.

1. Take off your gloves if you are wearing them.

2. Undo your chest-strap(s) — the harness will feel strange as the risers are now further apart but you will not fall out unless you lean right forwards.

3. If you have lots of time you can also slacken off your leg straps (you could even undo them if you remain supine).

4. Land as normal, but ensure that the canopy does not end up on top of you. This is best achieved in light winds by flaring very little. If there is a good breeze land cross or down wind and allow the canopy to fall in front of you. It will then stay full of air.

5. Wriggle out of or undo the leg straps. Try to avoid the lines.

6. If you are well away from land (after a line break from a boat tow

for example), you can use the canopy as a float by trapping air in the cells. It also acts as an efficient marker for any rescue attempt.

If you habitually fly near water carry a hook knife. These can slice through your risers or lines in seconds and free you if necessary. Avoid surf: it is probably better to land hard and PLF downwind on a beach than get caught in moderate surf as you could be tangled up and dragged around quite easily.

Tree landings. If you hit a tree, hit it hard and hang on. The main danger is falling out of it or getting pulled out by a gust of wind. Keep your legs together. Try to protect your eyes, turn your head or use one forearm. Gather in the canopy quickly if you are able to, or release yourself from it.

Power lines. Do not hit power lines. It is worth taking virtually any avoiding action including stalling at low level or crashing downwind to ensure you do not contact power lines. Two broken legs is far preferable to 40 per cent burns or death, both of which have been the result of hang gliders tangling with power lines in recent years. If "hung up" or assisting another pilot **wait** for the power to be cut off before attempting to get down or start helping.

Snow and heavy rain. Should it begin to snow or rain heavily while you are flying lose height and land as quickly as possible, as outlined in Chapter 9, Weather assessment. A weight of snow or water building up inside the trailing edge of the canopy can affect its flying characteristics and possibly cause an unrecoverable stall.

Flying in cloud. If you should find that a powerful cloud is sucking you upwards, the preferred method of losing height is a B line stall. If this is not available then a spiral dive. If this is ineffective the cloud must be a cu-nimb or strong wave. The up-currents and turbulence within clouds of this type can be severe. Induce a full stall and hold it until you have lost sufficient altitude.

Accidents

The best thing to do about accidents is avoid them! Most accidents are fortunately recorded and the statistics are published. Here is a summary of how to reduce hugely the chances of having an accident.

1. Get proper instruction.
2. Buy equipment the right size and skill level for you.
3. Only buy equipment with a Certificate of Airworthiness.
4. Do not fly in strong conditions until very experienced
5. Don't show off "hot dogging" near others or the ground.
6. Wear decent boots and a helmet (a back protector is recommended as well).
7. Do not attempt instability manoeuvres over land.
8. Do not take delivery of your new wing just before a trip to a new area or a competition. Get used to it on familiar territory.
9. Never take off from lower down a hill because it's too strong on top.
10. Take local advice.

11. Never fly to impress others or yourself.

12. Always pre-flight check and take good care of your equipment. Accidents do sometimes occur (often for one of the reasons above). If you suffer, or witness, an accident (or an "incident"), it is essential that you report it. The reasons are self-evident: if the national safety committee discovers that a large number of a certain type of canopy are involved in similar accidents or close shaves then it can take some action to prevent a repetition. If each incident is considered unimportant and ignored then obviously the problem will persist for much longer before coming to light.

The same applies to tightening up some aspect of training etc. An accident that is not reported promptly may also jeopardise any subsequent insurance claim. Your club safety officer or instructor will have report forms for this purpose.

Incidents that should be reported:
- Those involving any injury, either to pilot or a third party
- Those involving any damage
- Those in which an insurance or legal claim might arise
- Those in which any equipment failed to function
- Those involving use of non-standard procedures or training
- Anything that may highlight safety points or was unusual

Actions after an injury or fatality
- Administer first aid
- Call an ambulance / rescue services (mountain rescue can be reached through the usual emergency services number)
- Call police (essential if fatal)
- Do not disturb equipment
- Photograph any equipment and the area
- Take names and addresses of witnesses or bystanders. Inform the next of kin or ensure the police do so
- Inform the national association without delay. The numbers of the BHPA Safety and Development Officer and the Chairman of the Safety and Training Committee are published in the monthly magazine, *Skywings!*, or your instructor or club committee will have them.

Administering first aid

It is beyond the scope of this manual to cover all but the most basic first aid, but there are some practical points that are worth noting. Injuries generally fall into three categories.

● Slight, that is to say the injured person is not in any great danger. If there is any doubt at all these people should still be referred to hospital. Very often the shock of an injury and the wish to be OK makes the person belittle or not appreciate the damage. Many "sprained" ankles and "badly bruised" arms turn out to be fractured. Someone should always stay with the patient until they are passed into someone else's care.

● Major injuries. Major fractures or a combination of injuries are dangerous, not only in themselves, but because shock — particularly out on a cold hillside for long periods — can kill. Administer first aid as far as possible. DO NOT attempt to move the patient and make sure that the emergency services are told about the location and injuries. If you need a helicopter ask for one. Do not wait for the services to get there before saying "oh by the way we are up that mountain miles from the road". If you are in a remote location, station people at the road/track junction to help direct the ambulance to you. A canopy offers insulation and excellent protection from the elements. If a helicopter is called for, make sure that the area is cleared of unpacked canopies etc. One left out and well weighted down with stones is a useful marker.

● Extremely serious/fatal accidents. In addition to the steps above you must contact the police and the BHPA straight away. Do try to take photos of the site and the equipment. Do not disturb any equipment, if possible. The police will want to see it "in situ". Make sure that the names and addresses of witnesses are taken (bystanders as well as other pilots).

Important basics

A.B.C. This stands for airway breathing and circulation which are your priorities.

A. Make sure the casualty's airway is clear (head back, neck extended, chin lifted), and obstructions — teeth etc removed.

B. Check for breathing: if they are not, do it for them (mouth to mouth). Pinch the nose, seal the mouth with yours and blow smoothly, the chest should inflate. Wait for it to go down and repeat. Do it slowly. One inflation every four seconds is about right.

C. Check carefully for a pulse in the neck — if there is not one try to start the heart. Place the heel of your hand about 2cm above the point the ribs join the breastbone and lean on the heart five times. Check again for a pulse. If there is still not one, do two more inflations of the lungs (to get some oxygen in) then 15 more heart compressions (to pump it round to the brain). Compressions should be about 80 per minute.

If a casualty is bleeding badly, then apply direct pressure by gripping the wound firmly. Elevate the wound as high above the heart as you can and get plenty of padding to try and stop the bleeding. Fluid loss is the prime cause of shock. If the casualty is lying on a hill or mountainside, or is obviously badly injured, do not attempt to move him unless it is necessary to keep him breathing, as he may have spinal injuries. Do not remove helmets. Keep him warm and if he is conscious try to keep him that way. Keep a note of his condition (level of consciousness, pulse etc) — it may help the medical services.

Many clubs run first aid courses. It is always useful to make an effort to attend one: there are few feelings worse than helplessness in a situation such as this.

Tow launching and launching on skis

Tow launching

Some training centres use towing by hand in order to give launch and landing practice or to "steepen" shallow slopes, but tow-launching is generally done using a boat, vehicle or winch to provide the motive power, and launches to over above 1,000 feet are commonplace. In the UK the tow-launching of both round and ram air canopies has been well established for several years, usually using a Land Rover or similar vehicle and a fixed line over land, or a boat with a fixed line over water. With the advent of soaring flight and lighter, better performing and less forgiving canopies, procedures have been altered somewhat to reflect the changes. Weak links are now commonly used to prevent overstressing (125kg is about correct for a tow pressure of around 100kg). Payout systems are often used to maximise height, and powered winches that work by exerting a constant pull towards them enabling the pilot to climb as they approach the winch. These latter can be easily used without the need for a long smooth runway.

By adding another element to the flying, in this case a pull of about one "G", towing places twice as much stress on the canopy, and there are more things that can go wrong. For example, if the canopy drifts to one side it could reach a situation where the towing force is actually pulling it sideways into the ground, rather like a kite that is poorly controlled. This is known as a "lockout". The consequences of a partial collapse or a stall while under tow are also more serious than in free-flight, and finally there are more people and more equipment just waiting to malfunction. For all these reasons tow-launching must only take place with tested and approved equipment and, most of all, with an experienced and qualified instructor/operator.

There are a range of checks that must be learnt, including the release mechanism, signals to the driver or operator and so on. Typically, there is a release mechanism at the pilot's end and an emergency release at the operator's end. The tension of the tow line is kept constant, either through a tensiometer or by an automatic process like a clutch. A typical tow launch in the UK usually follows a set pattern.

1. The canopy and the winch are pre-flight checked
2. The line is attached to the pilot's quick-release
3. The pilot tries a test release to check everything is OK
4. Reattach
5. The signaller tells the operator to "take up slack" (either by radio or by under-arm swings of a bat)
6. When the line is straight and some tension is established the pilot launches the canopy. When inflated and checked the pilot gives the

command to go (usually "all out" or "push"). This is passed on by the signaller (overhead swings of the bat). If the pilot (or anyone else) wishes to abort the launch he shouts "Stop" and the signal is a stationary vertical bat.

7.   The tension comes on, and after a couple of steps the pilot is lifted into the sky. When he is well clear of the ground the operator may increase power slightly to give a better climb rate.

8.   During the climb, the pilot uses small control inputs to keep in line with the tow-line. He can signal for more or less power or to be released should he wish. At any point, the operator can cut the power and, when the line goes slack, the pilot releases and flies down (or up if he can find lift!)

9.   As the line falls (supported by a small drogue 'chute), it is re-wound by the operator ready to be laid out for the next launch.

People have in the past attempted to launch by tying a rope to a fixed object and allowing the wind to " kite" them up. This is unbelievably dangerous and is a banned practice. The last person who tried it was discovered by the BHPA when the safety officer was asked to attend the inquest.

If you are a foot launch pilot thinking of towing for the first time, there are a few points that are worth checking. Ensure the canopy is fully inflated and flying straight before requesting the tow to commence at normal power. Keep glancing up to check the canopy as you launch. Be very careful not to use lots of brake at launch, you could stall or deep stall the canopy as it takes off which is a very difficult situation for both the pilot

Towing from the shores of Galilee, Israel (payout winch in the foreground).

115

and winch operator to deal with. Remember that the control pressure will be increased while you are under tow. Do not forget to check the line has gone when you have operated the release.

Air law also extends to tow launching — it could be a disaster if pilots started towing up to a couple of thousand feet from their local fields all over the country. It would only be a matter of time before low-flying aircraft flew into the invisible and unmarked lines. The Civil Aviation Authority has granted permission for towing activities at various locations throughout the UK (almost always airfields) to qualified groups. These groups or clubs may tow to the height stated on the permit, (usually a maximum of 2,000ft). Any towing from a site without CAA permission must still be by qualified personnel and is limited to 200ft AGL (60m). Permanent towing activities are marked on air charts. Any that are not so marked must display a large symbol like a double plus sign in the vicinity to warn aircraft. Because it is easy to gain substantial altitude while having no hill behind you, towing is an excellent way to be in a position to practise instability exercises. Over water is recommended until you have established some expertise.

Launching from skis

Paragliding was really born in the Alpine ski resorts and naturally some of the first pilots were skiers. On snowy mountainsides with little wind it is often not possible to run anyway, so skis allow a fast and effective way to become airborne.The technique is the same as for an Alpine launch, but great care must be taken not to ski over the lines. It is very easy to damage them with the edge of a ski, particularly if there are rocks beneath the snow or if it is icy. It is difficult to get any traction, so in order to pull the canopy up you require a reasonably steep slope — your body weight should then provide the forward force. A steep slope with snow and skis may make stopping difficult once you are committed, so be meticulous in laying out the canopy and in your checks. Be careful when moving the canopy about to keep the snow out as far as possible, if much snow gets inside, it can make the launch more difficult and, at worst, even affect the flying characteristics of the paraglider.

The landing area may well be without snow: some pilots land on skis anyway, some choose to take them off in mid-air and hang them somewhere. Think about it before you take off!

Tandem (two-person) flying   32

Tandem flying is great fun, and an excellent way to teach certain disciplines such as soaring and thermalling. For the experienced pilot it is a good way to share the sport, and it really adds to your own enjoyment to share the air, especially on smooth "boring soaring" days. Many pilots and instructors who have seen tandem operating have shown great interest in doing it themselves. Most manufacturers are now building tandem wings, and canopies carrying two people are becoming a routine sight on British hills.

So how do you go about becoming a tandem pilot?

First of all you need to obtain the tandem qualification, You must be a very experienced and careful pilot and you will need to pass a tandem assessment .

The assessment criteria include practical demonstrations of skills, correct briefings and a good understanding of the ramifications (practical, legal and political!) of flying two people on one wing. There are some pre-conditions to applying for a UK tandem assessment: you must be a full annual member of the BHPA, have logged 100 hours (or 100 tows for tow pilots), hold the "pilot" rating and have flown at least 12 tandem flights with an existing tandem rated pilot (or under the supervision of a tandem instructor). Two of these flights must be in the student position. The BHPA, or any centre offering a tandem course, can provide details of precisely what is required.

This qualification is VITAL otherwise your insurance (BHPA or otherwise) will not be valid, and if you should have an accident flying tandem, consequences both for yourself and the whole sport could be catastrophic.

The law in the UK states that there must be no commercial gain unless the P2 (passenger) is on a proper course of instruction.

If you wish to fly children make sure you are still within the canopy's specified weight range, ensure you get written parental consent and exercise extreme caution.

If the flight is part of a course, the pilot must be an instructor, and the P2 must be a member of the BHPA and enrolled in the rating system. This is the ONLY way that tandem flights can take place if any money is involved. P 2's should usually be fit enough to cope with flight themselves. If you wish to fly a disabled person you should first contact the BHPA office for advice.

There are some technical considerations too. A very light P2 will tend to move up and may obscure the pilot's vision. The change in relative positions may also mean that you cannot reach the 'ears' either. Very tall P2's may make launch difficult. If in doubt try a small hop first.

It is vital that for safe operation another experienced pilot is present to act as anchorman, helper and to pre-flight the P2's equipment. For practical and insurance reasons this should be a BHPA member.

The equipment

To fly tandem safely you need specialised equipment:

— a purpose-made wing which is ACPUL or Guteseigel rated for tandem use.

— a spreader bar system that places the P2 slightly lower and in front of the pilot to prevent them being squashed together. (A good tandem canopy should come with this fitted).

— a full-face helmet is preferable for the pilot —your chin will be perhaps 25cm above and behind the P2's helmet and even a good landing could easily result in contact.

— a tandem reserve is a mandatory requirement.

— a spine protector is a good idea for the pilot as even a gentle stumble backwards will mean the other person's weight can fall on you as well.

The site and conditions

Flying tandem does impose a few restrictions on your choice of take-off and landing site. It is very difficult to move forwards over flat or uphill ground. A sharp edge is also a problem as the P2's weight leaving the ground first will pull you and the wing forward. If you haven't sufficient pressure in the wing at this stage the launch could be dangerous. Ideally you need a shallow slope falling away to a steeper one. This also helps with the actual inflation technique and if you are flying multiple P2s speeds your turnround time.

The conditions you can fly tandem in are much the same as usual. I have happily launched and landed in nil wind with a 190kg payload. If you are top landing you need to be certain you are not drifting backwards at all as with four legs to co-ordinate a quick twist and run is not practical. Turbulence is of course worrying to a non-flying P2 but certainly with the tandem wings I have used used the extra wing loading makes the wing feel more solid than a solo canopy.

Technique

The P2 must be properly briefed about what to expect. His or her equipment must be pre-flighted by an experienced helper. They must know how long the flight is expected to last, where you are expecting to land and that they must not fully depress the brakes or make violent inputs when they have control.

Above all they must know not to sit down or stop running during launch until they are told to do so by the pilot.

It is quite possible for the P2 to face forward while the pilot does a cross-brake reverse launch. This is perhaps the most useful method in the

Tandem at Plan Joux Chamonix — spot the hazard!

Take off later the same day in rather safer conditions.

119

UK where you are likely to be launching in gentle soarable winds. But, if the canopy does not come up straight, this can be problematical as you cannot easily sidestep to make a correction . In stronger soarable winds where you may come off the ground as you reverse launch an assisted alpine launch can be used, but you do need a competent helper for this.

In lighter winds if the slope is shallow I prefer to run side by side so that we can move faster without the risk of tripping over each other. (If this is likely to be the usual launch conditions then a modified spreader system can be used to make running side by side easier.) The crossed brake reverse launch technique is identical to a solo launch except that, because of the position of the passenger, one riser is much further away from you than the other. You must compensate for this as you pull up. It is easy to do provided you are already fluent with this launch technique solo.

During flight all movements should be progressive and the pilot should tell the P2 everything he is doing and why. If all is well when they have plenty of room the instructor may hand over control to the student keeping his own hands just above theirs so that he can guide or restrain any inputs if necessary. Within 5 minutes most people can fly around with no trouble. (I use the term instructor here because to hand over control introduces an element of instruction). If the pilot is not an instructor any incident or problem while the P2 has control would probably put them on very shaky legal ground.

I always use the aviation terminology "I have control" or "You have control" to prevent any confusion. Do not let the pilot under instruction try spiral dives or any similar manoeuvre, and BE CAREFUL — because of their lower position a tandem set up for the pilot to fly will mean they may need to fly with the brakes near their ears. Talk all the time. It is very reassuring and you can tell by the way they talk back (or not) if they are happy or tense. Warn them in plenty of time of impending glider wash or any manoeuvre you are doing and make sure they sit forward in their seats in time for landing.

If you are top landing in a good breeze you must have a helper to grab you as it is easier to fall over and harder to stop a 40m canopy drag-ging you. When teaching I find it best keep the flight to no more than 15 minutes. I usually aim to land on a slight slope so that I can launch again without moving. For best results teaching the brakes should be long enough for the student to use normally, of course this means you will often have to launch and fly with a wrap. You will find the control pressures are greater than usual (particularly the flare) so be prepared to take a couple of wraps to land and give yourself a rest every three flights or so.

A word of caution, it is not unknown for people to claim to want a tandem flight even when they are really very nervous about the idea (this includes your own wife/husband/girlfriend/children and mother!).

Before launch do take a minute to look them in the eyes and ask them (alone) whether they are happy about it. This is especially true when taking a group as peer pressure can be a hazard. If you have doubts then make an excuse and don't do it.

Tandem paragliding: qualifications

Proposals for the implementation of a tandem pilot qualification. (Self launch).

OPERATIONS

It is recommended that one other person , who should be a BHPA member, be present at the launch point to assist.

EQUIPMENT

Requirements

a. Only paragliders certified by SHV, ACPUL or DHV for tandem operation may be used. They must be used with proper regard to the manufacturers stated weight range and other recommendations.

b. Each person must have a properly fitting harness and helmet.

c. Log books for tandem flights must be raised and maintained.

d. An emergency parachute of a suitable size is recommended.

Recommendations

e. A spreader bar system (of a type approved by the manufacturer) is recommended.

f. A full -face helmet for the pilot (if behind the passenger) is recommended.

PERSONNEL

a. Pilots in charge must be members of the BHPA.

b. All tandem pilots (P1's) must hold a tandem pilot rating.

c. Tandem flights may not be undertaken for hire or reward. ("Valuable consideration" is the CAA term and does not only mean cash! — except it forms part of a course of instruction and the P1 is a qualified instructor.

d. The P2 (passenger) should normally be in good health. In the case of disabled persons advice should be sought from the S & DO before attempting tandem flights.

e.Passengers below the age of 18 must have written parental consent

f. Passengers must not be under the influence of drugs including alcohol.

PRE REQUISITES

a.The candidate must have at least 100 hours logged airtime on self-launch paragliders OR at least 50 hours logged airtime on self-launch paragliders and either 50+ tow launched flights OR 50+ hours logged airtime on hang-gliders.

b.The candidate must be a current annual member of the BHPA.

c.The candidate must hold at least a pilot rating (Self Launch).

d.The candidate must have logged a minimum of 10 tandem flight with a qualified P1 as the passenger, or with another candidate under the supervision of a tandem instructor.

e. The candidate must have logged at least 2 tandem flights flying in the passenger position.

f. The candidate must be able to demonstrate effective launch and ground handling techniques with a tandem wing. (A HIGH standard is required for a variety of wind conditions — ie complete control throughout the launch and landing sequence.)

g. The candidate must be able to fluently conduct suitable pre-flight briefings.

REGISTRATION

Before acting as a P1 the pilot must be registered with the BHPA as a tandem candidate. A CFI's support is required for both registration and annual renewal of this rating.

ON-GOING TRAINING

Tandem pilots and candidates are reminded that they must remain in current practice, and on going training is necessary should they fly in differing conditions (alpine for example) or fly a different model of tandem wing or use a different harness arrangement.

EXAMINATIONS

a. An independent examination shall be carried out by a tandem examiner.

b. The examination application procedure is the same as that for Instructors ie

(i) The CFI makes the application.

(ii) The chief examiner allocates an examiner and a date. A fee is payable.

(iii) If successful the qualification is awarded and is renewable annually. (Renewals must be supported by a CFI and by log-book evidence of current practice)

c. The examination is to include a written question paper.

Note 1. In the case of Instructors the exam shall include assessment of the candidates understanding of the use of tandem as an instructional tool.

Note 2. The candidate is required to provide his or her own equipment for the examination.

Mountain flying and flying abroad   ③③

Before setting out to fly in completely unfamiliar territory it is always worthwhile seeking information from your fellow club members, or from the local pilots when you arrive. The more you know about the site and the region, the safer and more enjoyable the flying will be. Do not be in a hurry to be the first to launch — always wait and see what the local fliers are doing. Always ask before flying — they may be a local school, or the club may have specific rules about who can fly. A little courtesy costs nothing and could pay dividends in advice and help later on. All these points apply equally to flying nearer home, of course. Before flying abroad, always take out medical and repatriation insurance — the cost of a helicopter rescue and treatment in many parts of the world are chargeable and expensive!

If you are going up in a cable-car or similar always take your flying licence or membership card as some operators will not let you up the mountain without them. Do not take anything you cannot easily fly down with. A mountain is nothing but a large hill — some are ridge-soarable but others are simply used as launch points to contact thermals rising from the valley floor or sides. Because of their scale, mountains create their own "micrometeorology" — that is to say that the wind and thermal development may be influenced as much by the mountain itself as by the prevailing conditions.

An important example of this is the airflow patterns throughout the day (Fig 42). In the morning there may well be a gentle katabatic flow (downhill) as the cool air sinks from the mountain-top into the valley bottom. There is no point in rushing over to the other side of the mountain

NIGHT.

DAY.

Katabatic flow.   Anabatic flow.

Fig 42. Shows the effect of daytime heating and night time cooling on airflow in valleys.   123

An Alpine flight in the late morning. The sun is now beginning to heat the valley floor, the clouds are dissipating and the first thermals of the day should be forming.

A canopy in 'Big Ears' mode. The pilot has deliberately collapsed the wing tips by pulling in the outer 'A' lines. This technique increases the glider's sink rate and is useful when conditions become too strong.

as the flow will be the same there. It is not unusual to find cloud in the valley bottoms in the morning. As the sun climbs and the valley sides warm up (rocky areas facing the sun first), the air will start to rise up the mountain sides (Anabatic flow) out of the valley and may become soarable. *See Fig 42.* As the rocks and slopes warm up, the thermals grow more and more powerful and turbulent. In summer it is not advisable to fly at all in some regions when activity is strongest. As the sun sinks the convection gradually decreases and large weak thermals are found. This is a good time for the inexperienced pilot to get used to the site. As the day ends, the air becomes calm and the lift dies. This scenario is fairly typical of Alpine flying conditions.

Large mountains have several effects on the airflow and it is not unusual to find an apparent wind blowing up both sides of a large ridge. This can give a convergence effect that can be usefully employed to fly many kilometres along the ridge crests. The same effect means that often mountains facing in different directions can be soarable simultaneously.

Valley winds

If there is a wind blowing it may only be felt at the tops of the mountains as a light breeze. But in deep V-shaped valleys the mountains can have the effect of compressing and accelerating the flow, giving strong winds in the valley bottom — a kind of reverse wind gradient. The effect means that the valley bottom may well be the most turbulent area. Ask the local pilots, who will probably be going home. An approaching weather front will also tend to push up the valleys before it is noticeable at launch.

Foehn

Foehn is a term used to describe a wind condition that is found in the Alps. The Foehn is, typically, a wind blowing across, or out from, the mountain range. The airmass may lose moisture as cloud often forms on the upwind side of the peaks where the altitude causes the vapour to reach dew point and where it may sometimes fall as snow. This moving airmass can cause rotor effects in the valleys and wave formations above the peaks. It is generally considered dangerous to fly in these conditions — something similar occurs in mountainous areas throughout the world. Tell-tale signs are dry wind blowing in the morning and poor visibility at low level.

Flight planning from mountains

If there is a large drop there is a chance that the wind in the landing area will be different in speed and direction from that at launch. Always allow a large margin for error and approach your field with spare altitude. Approach by circling over the field to establish the strength and direction (by noting your drift). Air density reduces with height, so do not forget that your stall will occur at a higher speed and therefore launching in no wind at high altitude will require a faster run than normal.

㉞ Competition flying

Many pilots enjoy flying competitively and there is a range of events from club level up to world championships that are hotly contested.

A typical task might be to fly cross-country as far as possible or around a number of turn points and landing at a 'goal'.

Tasks like these test the pilot's skill and judgment in the most comprehensive way. Competition flying does carry a slightly increased risk, as pilots often push themselves further than they might otherwise and many pilots may be competing for a small area of lift.

Competitions may take the form of one versus all or, in large events, several groups. In the latter case there is a "cut" after the first few tasks so that only, say, 30 per cent of the pilots go through to the final contest. There may be tasks that are timed from take-off to landing but these are hard to marshal, so the usual method is a launch "window". This means that any competitor is free to launch at any time during the preset time window and the fastest, or furthest, wins. Judging exactly when to launch becomes a major part of the competition.The technique for winning tasks where you are flying with a group is to select the thermal that has the biggest (or best) group of pilots and stick with it. All you have to do is fly better than anyone else in your "gaggle" and you are assured of a reasonable placing. Of course someone unexpected may score better than you, but if you keep winning the "A" team gaggle, eventually you will come out on top or very near it.

Hints

Good equipment is vital, not only a canopy but a reliable camera (used to prove you have reached the turn points), instruments and a reserve. Know the rules! Competitions have been won (and lost) because only a few pilots realised the rules biased points in favour of speed over distance, or a target landing over speed etc. Do not rush — inexperienced competition pilots often fly too early. You must know the weather forecast to decide whether it will improve or not. You must also keep tabs on how you are doing in the competition — if you are not aware of everyone else's position as the competition progresses, you will not know who you should "target" in the tasks. Should you play safe? or should you go for it if you have nothing to lose? But don't forget, you are doing it for fun!

Instructor ratings

35

In Britain, most of the responsibility for selecting, training and using instructors lies with the Chief Flying Instructor (CFI) of a training centre. If you are interested in teaching you first need to approach a CFI and convince him that you have the right stuff to make an instructor. If he agrees you will be signed on as a Trainee Instructor (TI) and begin to help at the school. At this stage you can not take charge of students and must be under the supervision of a senior instructor, though if he thinks you are capable enough he may decide to take a larger group than usual. At this point (usually after a week or so) it is usual for the school to pay a nominal daily rate.

The next step is to attend a Trainee Instructor course. These are intensive two-day courses and cover all aspects of administration and instructional theory. After a period of working in the school and gaining experience, if your flying, instructing and first aid qualifications are suitable, and you have successfully completed the TI course, your CFI may put you forward for an examination. An exam takes all day and is conducted by an experienced instructor. You will be asked to do some hands-on training, demonstrate your flying skills, pass a theory exam, and have an interview. You will be informed whether you have passed or failed on the same day. If you have failed you will be told why, and advised either to reapply when the weak points are resolved, or not to reapply at all.

When you have amassed considerable experience as an instructor, including training inexperienced instructors etc you may apply for the Senior instructor rating. You will need to pass a another two day course which sets a high standard not only in instructing skills but also in the administration of a training centre. After a further examination day you may achieved Senior Rating which is a requirement for appointment as a CFI.

State of the art, innovations, the future

36

At the time of writing (January 96) the top performance canopies are offering a sink rate of around 1.1m per second. This is similar to the wings of the last two or three years, but the real improvement has come at the top end of the speed range: 50kph + top speeds and glide performance of 8.5:1 are now achievable and on these machines cross-country flights are becoming more and more commonplace. The world open distance record is currently 330km and even more notably the distance and average speed being achieved in international competition tasks is still climbing steadily. Perhaps the most important achievement, however, is that the wings aimed at the recreational pilots are now only a very small performance margin behind those of the top competition pilots and the safety and security offered by them far superior to that available just a few years ago.

In practice there are few radical innovations apparent at present. Perhaps the most notable is the move towards diagonal cell walls that has appeared recently. A diagonal rib allows a huge number of attachment points to the top surface giving a very smooth and clean airfoil. This is achieved without making the bottom of the cells any narrower and so gives improvement in performance without losing stability. Whether this will turn out to be a design step that proves durable or whether it will fade away like the mesh ribs or metal spreader bars that were once hailed as a significant improvement is hard to say. What is clear is that the computer aided design required to plot and cut such complex shapes is making it harder and harder for the small manufacturers to compete with the major players.

Over the last couple of years prototypes have been flown that are forward swept, contain spanwise battens, have air intakes on the underside of the wing and upward (or downward) "diffuser" tips. Many have ever decreasing numbers of lines!

A novel innovation seen recently is the paraglider without brakes. The "cage" is a French device that does away with risers and controls all together and relies on weight shift which is enhanced by the lines being connected directly to an aluminium framework which the pilot can tilt almost like a hang-glider control frame. Clearly this machine is heavier and more complex than existing designs and how the pilot is able to deal with collapses or other problems is not clear to me. It is good to know, however, that there are those out there who are constantly pushing the boundaries of what is possible in the sport.

Perhaps the most enduring and notable changes in the last couple of years have been not in the wings themselves but in the harnesses and instruments we fly with. Harnesses have evolved enormously and the addition of spinal protection systems has been a major change. Also, the inclusion of an airbag is now becoming a familiar safety device on various harnesses. On the instrument side, the revolution in navigation caused by the hand-held global positioning system has had a major impact. Cross-country pilots and others are also making more and more use of the digital revolution by carrying cellphones! (I recently overheard a pilot calling in from the hilltop to tell his boss he wouldn't make it back to the office today because he was stuck in traffic!)

Flying is one of mankind's oldest dreams, yet sport flying of any kind has always been an activity for a very few people. The cost, time and expertise required make almost any form of aviation impractical for most people. Yet paragliding makes flying affordable and achievable for a great many more. It is already established as a mainstream activity in many ski resorts. The advantages of a portable, easy-to-fly machine have already encouraged thousands of people to take to the air and the sport is still growing quickly. These colourful wings are steadily becoming a more common sight on our hills and mountains.

Cumulus skyscape

Liz Addy

· **Paramotors** ·

Paragliders were initially designed for unpowered soaring flight, but then so was Wilbur and Orville's first Wright flyer just about 100 years ago and like them the attraction of being able to fly from anywhere and not be dependent on the whims of the wind and thermals is very appealing to many modern pilots. It was inevitable then that as hang-gliding gave birth to microlighting, so paragliding would eventually lead to paramotoring.

In fact there are two paths that have been taken, the first is to reinvent the microlight trike configuration which gives easier ground control and has some operating advantages. (Though its size and weight has generally meant a special wing is needed and which must be de-rigged or trailered to move it.)

The second is the back-pack paramotor, which appeals very strongly to paraglider pilots because of its simplicity, small size and weight and because it can be used with a normal paraglider wing. The disadvantage here is that you must be able to fly a paraglider before you can use one and the ground handling and launch in some situations may demand a good degree of fitness, co-ordination and skill.

The trike type is perhaps the easiest with which to train new pilots and will best suit some of those who are exclusively interested in powered flight.

Back-packs (especially those with an air-restart capability) can be used both for powered flight and also as a way of getting up there for pilots who may then choose to switch off and thermal in the usual way. These are the most popular variant and this section is principally concerned with the back-pack type.

An introduction to the equipment

The paramotor consists of a lightweight engine (usually a 2 stroke) which is mounted on a rigid frame of steel or aluminium, and which drives a pusher propellor. The small fuel tank (up to 8 litres is usual) is also within the frame and the propellor is shielded from dangling lines and flung back arms and legs by a "cage" covered in a mesh of some kind to allow a free-flow of air whilst offering protection from the spinning propellor, rather like a giant household fan! Some engines are direct drive but many feature a reduction drive of some sort to optimise the propellor revolutions. The other side of the frame is fitted with connection points for the pilots harness so that the whole thing can be worn as a back-pack. (fig 43) Typical weight is around 14-30kg depending on type.

The engines are chosen for lightness, good fuel consumption, reliability and suitable power output. The result is that the same few models are incorporated into many different paramotors. Typically they are from 125cc up to around 300cc. A usable power output for a pilot who wishes to be able to launch from flat ground is around 15BHP. Though

Northern Paragliding

Paramotor pilot preparing for launch — note over-shoulder hang-points and ear defenders.

131

Below: A paramotor pilot prepares to reverse launch.

Inset: A fellow flyer looks on incredulously "You cannot be serious!" (Photographs: Northern Paragliding)

some smaller units designed principally for sustaining flight may generate as little as 7BPH .

The thrust is perhaps more dependent upon the propellor used than the actual engine and prop choice is one of the major design factors in manufacturing a paramotor (one designer apparently tested over 35 props before settling on the final design). And thrust is only one consideration. It may be easy to increase it with a larger propellor, but this also has implications for the torque effect applied to the pilot and the noise level generated — if the propellor tips become supersonic the resulting increase in noise levels can be significant.

Most paramotors use a wooden propellor with a diameter of between 90 and 130cm. Two, three of four blades may be used but this is often more a function of reducing noise levels than for additional thrust. Wood is a favoured material because it is light, not too expensive, and can resist minor damage like stone chips etc. It is also somewhat safer in an accident as the blades will shatter on first impact whereas metal or carbon fibre blades may remain intact and could therefore do more damage. The other half of this equation is that composite or metal propellors can be manufactured in more radical swept shapes which may be of benefit in noise reduction and in reducing diameter and of course they are more damage resistant.

The frame and cage are most frequently of aluminium although stainless steel has been used, especially on the very smallest units were the additional weight is tolerable. Fibreglass or carbon fibre rod has also been used for the outer rim of the cage as this has the great advantage of being bendable and so can be disassembled and packed into a small space. It may also be less likely to sustain damage from being dropped than an aluminium rim.

Most manufactures offer a choice of size . The larger units with bigger props give more power but need a much bulkier cage. These may then have to be disassembled for transport. The tiny ones may not get off flat ground with a heavier pilot but are of course more compact.

All paramotors can be started with a recoil starter (pull handle), in the same way as a lawnmower or chainsaw, but because the compression is relatively high this is very difficult if not impossible to do whilst wearing the paramotor (ie flying!) A very useful feature on any unit (particularly for the soaring or fuel conscious pilot) is an air restart. This can be a decompressor to allow an easier pull or, more commonly, an electric start of some type.

The throttle control is typically a "squeeze for power" hand unit. These are initially rather awkward whilst ground-handling as the same hand is simultaneously controlling a brake, but with practice most pilots master the technique. The throttle incorporates a kill switch so that the engine can be stopped at anytime during the launch or flight if a problem occurs. Because any slip or stumble on landing could result in considerable damage if the prop contacts the ground or the wing collapses onto the spinning prop, landings are typically made "dead stick" ie with the engine off.

At least one design features a centrifugal clutch which means the engine is disengaged from the propellor whilst the pilot is ground-handling, landing, or even just putting the paramotor on his back. Once the wing is fully inflated and overhead the throttle is applied engaging the clutch and spinning the prop for launch. This system has obvious safety advantages.

Another important design factor is the connection of the back-pack to the risers of the wing. There are three usual alternatives. The first is to use attachments on the main lift webbing of the harness as usual. These need to be very high towards the shoulders as a low centre of gravity will cause the weight of the paramotor to tilt the pilot onto his back.This is simple but makes the harness harder to get into and is not particularly comfortable.

The second method is to use a low C of G as normal but to compensate for the weight at the pilot's back by using small extensions to the frame. This lets the attachment points move fore and aft and also allows the harness to be hung from a slightly further forward position on the frame to balance the motor weight. This is a good solution for paraglider pilots as the ground handling of the machine is much more "normal" — the brakes are in the same position as for free-flight and the big ears etc are easy to reach. However, because there is rather less pendular stability the torque of the prop, especially at high revs, is much more noticeable.

The third solution is to use "over the shoulder" frame extensions (fig X) which make the harness easy to use and yet minimise torque. This system is popular with those who are concerned principally with powered flight and works best with powerful units and larger diameter propellors. Ideally the harness should feature a diagonal cross-brace strap to minimise torque.

NB: The higher than normal attachment points means that a standard paraglider requires the control lines to be lengthened. This may make reaching the lines for Big Ears impractical and, in some cases, it is possible that a short pilot may not be able to reach the brakes at the keepers if they are released. Check these points before take-off!

Aerodynamic considerations

Weight: A paramotor is quite heavy — at around 20kg it contributes perhaps 20 per cent of the payload on the wing. The first question then is what wing-loading is acceptable to the canopy, and do we therefore need to fly a larger wing than usual to accommodate the increase?

To answer that question we need to consider how the recommended loadings were arrived at originally. Most manufacturers agree that the wing loadings for free flight are designed to offer the best sink-rate performance possible without sacrificing stability and recovery behaviour in unstable situations. If the paramotor is intended to simply be a means to "get up there" and then thermal or otherwise free-fly then clearly it is advisable to ensure the total payload is within the optimum free-flight range to give the best performance. If, however, the whole aircraft is principally to be used under power when the paramotor is connected then sink-rate becomes less important and a smaller wing may be better in many ways offering enhanced handling speed and stability. Of course, the ultimate load is important too and the manufacturer's maximum load placarding must not be exceeded. (Some manufacturers do test to beyond the optimum loadings given in the manuals — you will need to check on their recommendations concerning paramotors.) If you do use the same wing for powered and unpowered flight it is important to realise that brake settings may need to be adjusted and that landing speeds will be somewhat higher with the greater payload of a motor on board. The additional weight of the motor is, of course, not evenly distributed; it is all on the pilot's back. This means that a paramotor system requires a re-think of the hang-point placement as mentioned above and also needs care in landing as a poor touchdown may have worse consequences than if free flying.

Thrust: By adding thrust we alter the forces acting upon the aircraft. It is now possible to fly faster at a high angle of attack, for example. The main effect of this is, of course, the ability to be able to climb when there is no lift, but it is important to understand that thrust can alter the behaviour of the wing in certain circumstances. For example: adding power in a turn can steepen the angle of bank considerably.

Torque: Sir Isaac Newton was the first person we know to state the "equal and opposite reaction" law of motion. Unfortunately for him he never had the opportunity to try it out on a paramotor. If he had have done he would no doubt have been gratified by the obedience of the paramotor to this principle and would have understood the problem of torque — ie because the propellor is spinning one way the rest of the aircraft will try and spin the other. It cannot, of course, because of the far greater mass and inertia, but the effect is still felt as a tendency for the wing to turn in the opposite direction to the prop's rotation. With a large prop, or at high revs, this force can be quite acute and make turning against it, or even maintaining course, quite difficult. This problem is minimised by the addition of a diagonal "anti-torque" strap to the harness.

Piloting considerations

Back-pack paramotors are great fun to use and are certainly the most compact and portable powered aircraft on Earth. However, like almost all designs they are a compromise of many conflicting design criteria, and in addition to the complications of adding power to the aerodynamic equation we should also consider the effect upon the piloting requirements.

Launch

A paramotor can be launched in the same two basic ways as an unpowered canopy. It is generally done with the engine already warmed and running on tickover.

If there is a little wind then the reverse launch is probably a better bet as the additional weight makes falling on your backside a distinct possibility if alpine launching. This is bad news for the propellor and can be embarrassing if you should finish up in the aptly named "turtle" position. The technique is almost the same as for regular reverse launching except that great care must be taken not to "blip" the throttle and with over shoulder hang-points a good pull may be required as you can only reach half way up the front risers. If you are not used to launching on flat ground, be warned that the paraglider may need a hefty pull anyway as the tendency to drop back will be more marked. Choice of wing is quite important here.

If there is little or no wind, you will require an alpine launch: again a good pull is required and to prevent stalling or overflying you must be able to run fast enough to keep the wing solidly inflated and controllable above you until the power kicks in. This can be quite hard as the natural inclination is to lean forward, but if the position is too exaggerated then the thrust will drive you down rather than along. Once inflated and powered up, your unit should have sufficient power to lift you cleanly and strongly off the ground in just a few paces. Trying to launch underpowered systems is quite amusing for the spectators but no fun for the pilot! Do not retract your undercarriage until well clear of the ground! During the launch procedure the thumb should be poised over the kill switch to stop the prop if anything goes wrong.

As your strides lengthen and you apply more power you will find that the torque is driving you slightly off line. Whilst you can compensate to some degree with the brakes it may not be possible to hold the wing perfectly straight. For this reason your launch "runway" should have adequate space to allow some deviation.

In flight

Flying a paramotor is virtually the same as a canopy in free-flight, with the slight complication that it prefers turning in one direction to the other. The addition of thrust also means that the angle of attack is raised slightly and that the throttle can be used in addition to the brakes and weight shift for manoeuvring.

Foot or hand-operated speed systems are very useful as they can be used to offset the sometimes unwanted increase in angle of attack created by adding throttle. Most wings actually reduce their airspeed as the motor reaches higher revs for this reason.

Big ears is less useful than on a free-flight wing as its principal function is to combat strong lift and the paramotor is generally flying in neutral air. High hang-points may mean that the lines are too inaccessible to allow it anyway.

As a new paramotor pilot I found that my tendency was to treat the motor as something that might pack up at any moment, which is perhaps not a bad thing. Having witnessed experienced pilots turning down wind at almost zero altitude and then climbing away it became apparent that some had more faith than I! It has demonstrated that the free-flight pilot's first reaction to cut the throttle in a stressful situation is not always the best thing to do — flying under power does require a slightly different mind set.

Instability situations

A paramotor is really a light wind machine. In horizontally moving air any paraglider is hard pressed to make much upwind progress and a powered wing is no exception. For this reason they are not generally flown in strong wind conditions. However, it is perfectly possible to use the motor to put yourself above previously unreachable terrain, flying up a narrow valley for example, or contacting high altitude wave. Of course thermal activity may still be encountered and may cause closures of the wing.

Because the motorised wing is likely to be more heavily loaded than in free flight it will retain a high degree of stability. However, the additional weight and the complication of thrust may work against you in some situations, such as a spin. The best advice if conditions become rough is to escape the area as soon as possible, which may well mean a forced landing. In the event of non-critical asymmetric closures it is preferable to keep the power on whilst you clear the tuck if at all practical. In serious instability situations however it is better to cut the power. This is not only to reduce any effect of thrust and torque but also to reduce the noise — the first indication of a problem is often the sound of the wing fluttering, and under power this is impossible to detect.

Tucks etc should be dealt with in the same way as for free-flight by maintaining course and pumping out the collapse.

Noise

Because the groundspeed of a canopy is so low, the noise from the motor lingers for some time. Though not noisy at all by aircraft or even microlight standards the paramotor does have a very large "acoustic footprint." At the time of writing the Ministry of Transport has yet to impose a maximum noise level on these machines, but it seems inevitable that they eventually will, as is already the case with microlights in the UK. To minimise the noise for residents of your launch area it is important to vary your flight patterns, and to avoid high revs at low altitudes. The very portability of the machine should make using a selection of different launch sites feasible. Noise affects the pilots too and ear defenders are certainly a good idea for prolonged flights. Maintaining altitude at minimum revs is the most comfortable way to fly!

Landings

As a general rule landings should be made "dead stick" — with the power off — to minimise the risk of damage in the case of a trip or slip. A slightly untidy or stumbling landing in free-flight can translate to a nasty fall or even a broken prop when paramotoring, as the additional weight of the unit can make keeping footing more difficult. Good landings are essential, so ensure your landing area is suitable and that your approach is accurate. There is no excuse for losing the wind direction with a paramotor as you have the facility to examine the area and fly a complete circuit to establish drift before entering your final leg.

If you are flying a small and heavily loaded wing a strong and well timed flare is a skill you will need to have practised!

㊳ Learning to fly a paramotor

What will a paramotor training course consist of ? In the UK at the time of writing such courses are still in their infancy and the precise content and standard of the qualification still being refined. The proposed syllabus below has been arrived at by the BHPA development and training panels with some input from the British Microlight Aircraft Association (BMAA) plus one or two additions of my own. It is very likely to reflect the content of UK training courses for those with some paragliding background. The Ab-intio (complete beginner) student who wishes to learn paramotoring will at present need to undertake a short period of unpowered paragliding training and it is likely to prove that this will remain the case. If this is your situation I strongly recommend that your paragliding tuition is tow (winch) based as this is much more akin to the situation and effects that you will experience when you strap on a motor. Much hill flying is concerned with using lift and the peculiarities of flying in proximity to a slope. 360 turns and circuits are not a feature of early hill training for example.

Theory

Show an appropriate understanding of the following topics.

1. The Power unit
1.1.1. Configuration including two-stroke operation
1.1.2 Mixing fuel

1.1.3 Safety
1.1.4 Starting procedures
1.1.5 Power generated torque effects
1.1.6 Running in
1.1.7 Hang-points (effects of altering)
1.1.8 Weight checks

2. Power checks
1.2.1 Clearing the fuel supply of bubbles
1.2.2 Clear prop
1.2.3 Cut off switch
1.2.4 Power on

3. Theory of flight
1.3.1 Thrust and drag
1.3.2 Forces in turns
1.3.3 Climbing and diving turns
1.3.4 Reduction drives
1.3.5 Propellor theory

4. Taking off
1.4.1 Choice of safe field including climb out clearance, ground
conditions and turbulence generators
1.4.2 Assessment of conditions
1.4.3 Safe areas for onlookers
1.4.4 Noise nuisance
1.4.5 Torque effects
1.4.6 Methods of inflation
1.4.7 The run. Use of brakes
1.4.8 Emergency stopping (launch abort)

5. Flight
1.5.1 Torque effects
1.5.2 The micrometeorology likely to be found in XC situations.
Valley winds, rotors etc.
1.5.3 Speed systems The effects on a powered paraglider.
Power on and power off situations.
1.5.4 Techniques for avoiding and recovering form tucks, stalls and
spins
1.5.5 Navigation exercise. The student will plan a 30km (total)flight
either as an out and return with a predeclared turnpoint or as a
flight to a declared goal.

6. Flying rules
1.6.1 Congested areas
1.6.2 Noise nuisance

1.6.3 Flying over water

7. Air Law
1.7.1 Aeronautical charts,
1.7.2 Restricted and prohibited airspace,
1.7.3. Line features , Quadrangle rule
1.7.4 VMC minima
1.7.5 CANP system
1.7.6 Radio considerations

8. Landing
1.8.1 Power on/off
1.8.2 Kill switch management
1.8.3 Light wind/high wind situations.
1.8.4 Effects of weight on flying speed. Stall speed and flare.

Practical

Demonstrate the following in an effective/competent manner.

1. Pre-flight
2.1.1 Perform an effective PLF (not wearing a back-pack)
2.1.2 Canopy ground handling
2.1.3 Launch assisting
2.1.4 Pre-take off control of the paramotor
2.1.5 Post landing control of the paramotor
2.1.6 Parking the paramotor

2. Flight
The student will perform the following tasks to the satisfaction of the instructor.

2.2.1 Three consecutive powered flights from a flat site with at least 100ft ground clearance with unassisted take off runs, smooth 90 degree turns to left and right and stand up landings

2.2.2 Demonstrate a short field landing by landing within 40 metres of an imaginary 5 metre high obstruction

2.2.3 Complete 3 landings within 10m of a defined spot in winds of less than 5mph

2.2.4 Complete 3 landings within 10m of a defined spot in winds of more than10mph

2.2.5 Minimum of 10 paramotor flights logged including full deflation and inflation of wing between flights.

2.2.6 Demonstrate safe and effective use of rapid descent technique (not B riser stall)

2.2.7 Maintain directional control and show recovery from tucks of between 20 per cent and 30 per cent

2.2.8 Carry out power-off landings to the satisfaction of the instruc
tor from various heights some of which are over 500ft

2.2.9 Show knowledge of forward and reverse launches and
demonstrate them

2.2.10 Complete a 30km (total) flight with a pre-declared goal

Competence and experience

1. Competence

The student will demonstrate competence of the following topics to
the satisfaction of the instructor.

3.1.1 Consistently demonstrate safe airspeed control

3.1.2 Safely demonstrate slow flight awareness and discuss
symptoms and dangers (deliberate stalls must be avoided)

3.1.3 Demonstrate an ability to fly co-ordinated 360 degree turns in
both directions

3.1.4 Display the ability to fly safely with others maintaining a good
lookout complying with the Rules of the Air and exhibiting
good airmanship. Demonstrate an ability to manoeuvre the
paramotor safely considerately and in accordance with air
traffic rules.

2. Experience

Prior to being certified as a paramotor pilot and/or flying outside
direct visual range of the training field other than to execute to specific
training task, the student must satisfy the instructor regarding the following and, where required, furnish the appropriate evidence.

3.2.1 Passed the BHPA PPG exam

3.2.2 Must have successfully flown paramotors or paragliders or
hang-gliders or microlights on at least 8 separate days within
the previous 9 months

3.2.3 Must have a minimum of 5 hours logged airtime on
paragliders, hang-gliders or microlights of which at least 3
hours must be on paramotors

3.2.4 Satisfy the instructor that the pilot has correct attitude to
continue a flying career both safely and competently

Much of the subject matter mentioned here is not covered in this
book. However, we have plans to produce a paramotor guide as well and
wherever you purchased this volume should be able to supply you with
information of the more detailed publication *"Paramotoring": a complete
guide.*

Training course

An actual training course is likely to conform to the following basic
pattern.

At groundschool you will be introduced to the equipment and learn about safety checks and procedures and watch the instructor demonstrate what a paramotor is capable of. This will include airfield discipline, the importance of correct clothing, (even simple things like long hair or a drawstring on a jacket can be drawn into a rotating prop), mechanical checks and dealing with spectators etc. If the school has a static simulator you may then have the opportunity to hang up in a paramotor and try it out, learning to respond to radio commands and just get the feel of the unit on your back. Launch is the critical phase of flying one of these machines, and some time will be given over to practising forward (alpine) launches. If the school is using a winch for pre-motorised flights you will then have an opportunity for low unpowered flights to get used to basic control of the wing, working up over a couple of days to towing a reasonable height and flying a good circuit with a dummy motor on your back. This stage can be reached almost straight away if you have some free-flying experience.

Mixed in with these exercises will be a fair bit of theory, covering much the same ground as a free-flight Club Pilot with additional sections on air law and, of course, the use of power.

Very soon it will be time for your first paramotor flights and you will soon be buzzing around the field practising co-ordinated turns, dead stick (power off) landings, maintaining level flight etc. You will also cover subjects such as reducing noise nuisance, rapid descents (big ears), dealing with small trucks, reverse launching and be able to demonstrate accurate landings. Once your instructor is satisfied you have absorbed sufficient information and expertise, it is time for your 30km cross-country navigation exercise.

The 'Navex' will mean you must decide on the suitability of the weather, calculate your approximate ground speed and fuel consumption and be able to navigate either by compass bearing, ground features or even GPS to a prearranged goal. Very often this will mean flying an out and return pattern or perhaps triangular course. It may mean avoiding airspace of some type. Your instructor may or may not follow you depending on his or her level of confidence!! If you can successfully manage this task and convince your instructor you are suitably competent and have a good safe attitude, it remains only to pass the theory exam paper, for which you should now be well prepared.

I personally anticipate that a non-pilot will take around nine days to achieve this level and I know other very experienced instructors in the UK and other countries concur. Beware of anyone who sems keen to sell you a paramotor and tells you that you can be trained in much less time!!

For a pilot with experience in a related discipline — especially paragliding this time could be as little as two or three days.

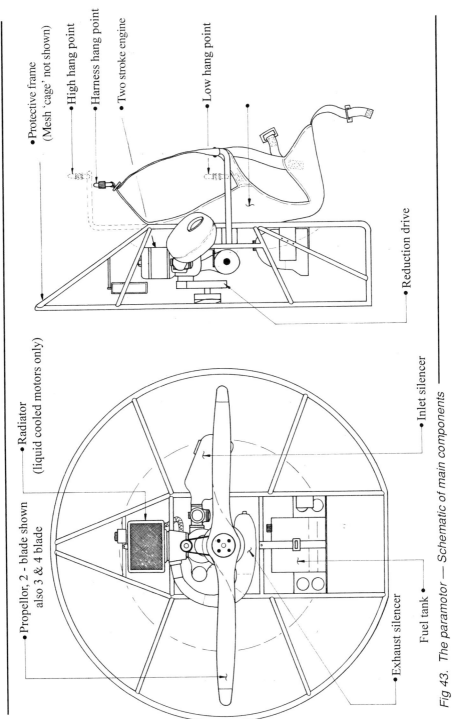

• Protective frame
(Mesh 'cage' not shown)

• High hang point

• Harness hang point

• Two stroke engine

• Low hang point

• Reduction drive

• Radiator
(liquid cooled motors only)

• Inlet silencer

• Propellor, 2 - blade shown
also 3 & 4 blade

• Exhaust silencer

• Fuel tank

Fig 43. The paramotor — Schematic of main components

143

FOOT LAUNCHED POWERED AIRCRAFT (FLPA)
Code of Practice

Preamble

This code of practice has been written in mid-1996 as FLPA are being de-regulated. There has been some justified concern by other fliers that the unrestrained use of FLPA may jeopardise other free flyers which is why this document has been drafted.

Scope and authority

This document is intended to give general guidance and unless stated its contents are not mandatory. However, it should be noted that where disputes arise which lead to legal action, non compliance may be detrimental.

Mandatory requirement

All FLPA pilots should comply with the spirit and the letter of the General exemption and all relevant Air Law.

Association requirements

In addition to mandatory requirements the BHPA and BMAA may introduce regulations from time to time. Pilots should maintain their membership of one of the Associations and keep up to date with existing and new regulations and guidance. If you are not a member of BMAA or BHPA you should join and obtain a pilot rating. If you become involved in legal action in the future, proof of you skills and knowledge via your pilot rating will be an advantage.

Taking off — general

Wherever possible FLPA should take off from a recognised and/or secure area. The ideal situation is an existing microlight airfield which has the appropriate Local Authority permissions.

When pilots take off from existing microlight areas they should familiarise themselves with and comply with local rules.

If the FLPA takes off from other areas the following procedures should be taken.

— The area should be secure from the possibility of animals and/or spectators being in an area of damage (note: a shattered propeller can scatter sharp shards of wood at high speed).

— Any spectators should be properly marshalled and any dogs should be firmly attached to a lead (they have been known to chase the FLPA when it starts to move).

— The take-off area should be closely inspected for possible trips and holes.

— Proper permission should be obtained from the owner of the land.

— Any neighbours should be warned of your future activities.

Taking off — planning approval

Unless the land is in a special zone such as a conservation area you can usually fly from a temporary take-off area on 28 days in any 12 months. If you fly on more than 28 days without Planning Approval the owner of the land may be served with an enforcement notice by the Local Authority and could be subject to a fine. Local Authorities will generally include all of the land in one ownership in an enforcement order so don't try to argue that you are taking off from different fields and they each have a 28 day dispensation (it is this smart Alec attitude that this document is seeking to avoid). The Local Authority may also have local byelaws which should not be contravened.

Taking off — nuisance

Even if you comply with the Planning Regulations you may fall foul of the law of nuisance. For a prosecution to take place there must be evidence that the nuisance has occurred on an regular basis. A video of you taking off ten days in succession at 6am very close to a house could result in a large fine and the confiscation of your aircraft.

Taking off - hang gliding and paragliding sites

Don't — unless you have permission from the club.

Flying — general

If you take off from one place, vary your flight path to avoid annoying the general public.

In particular, powered paragliders flying against the wind will remain in view for a long period of time. If they fly higher to make less noise they will fly slower due to the wind gradient. If you are not making much headway it may be safer to land and get a lift back to base.

It should be noted that German research has shown that an aircraft is a greater source of annoyance if it can be seen.

Flying — hang gliding and paragliding sites

It will be very tempting to buzz your mates who are grounded on a nil wind day. Don't.

A number of hang gliding and paragliding clubs have introduced rules which generally exclude FLPA and in at least one case there is a self-declared exclusion zone round each site. FLPA pilots from BHPA and BMAA cannot be expected to be conversant with every rule introduced by clubs participating in other types of flying. However, where such a rule is known to exist it should be respected.

The general rule to be followed is 'use your common sense and stay away.

Flying — livestock

Adherence to the General Exemption should mean that livestock is not disturbed. However, you should particularly avoid bird sanctuaries and riding stables. If you are taking off from a field you should check that there are no horse riders in the vicinity. If there are — wait.

Landing

For a variety of reasons you may decide to 'land-out'.

If you are landing on private land you should **always** find the landowner and tell him/her of your arrival. Courtesy takes five minutes of your time and invariably results in a pleasant experience. One pilot always carries a miniature bottle of scotch with him to offer to the landowner which is always accepted with amusement and gratitude (it's the thought that counts!)

Display flying

Display flying should be undertaken only after seeking and being granted permission by a Display Evaluator appointed by CAA. BMAA or BHPA head office will be able to give you the names of Display Evaluators.

Conclusion

Any breach of common sense or good manners is a breach of this Code of Practice. Please remember that the General Exemption has been issued on a temporary basis.

• REFERENCE SECTION •

Passing your exams

Most countries require their pilots to pass some form of written theory exam before qualifying as a pilot. There are several reasons for this — the most obvious to ensure that each pilot has sufficient knowledge to fly at the chosen level safely. Exams, when properly debriefed, also educate the pilot, allow the instructor to check their own thoroughness, strengths and weaknesses, and when collated by the national association help pinpoint areas that require particular attention.

Preparation

It need not be a struggle to absorb the information you need. Paragliding is something we do for fun and have an interest in, and so the theoretical aspects can be related to real events or experiences. It may be hard to recall what cloud type occurs where, but recalling how the sky looked that day when you first found yourself thousands of feet off the ground should not be too hard. Be aware of the level you are aiming at. It is not much use answering an advanced pilot question about the development of a thermal by saying "hot air rises". Equally a student pilot level question about stability will not require a critique of design factors. Your instructor should brief you about what level to expect.

Taking the exam

— If you are not ready don't take it. Ask your instructor to ask a few similar questions first if you are not sure you are prepared. If it is a long exam, particularly for one of the higher levels, make sure that you are not tired, wet or hungry before you start. In other words do not sit the exam straight after getting in from a day's flying.

— Make sure you have the correct equipment, some exams may require a calculator or a ruler.

— Read the instructions! In a multiple choice exam set recently the instructions clearly stated that one or more answers may be correct but the majority of pilots still failed to tick more than one box even though it transpired that they knew two options were right!

— Allow plenty of time. Make sure you have sufficient time to do the exam in the longest period allowed and some spare to go over it afterwards with your invigilator.

If the invigilator is a club volunteer or an instructor staying on late to help you out don't forget to buy them a beer!

In the UK the exams are set by the BHPA and are all multiple choice papers. The topics you will need to know are:

Student pilot
— Rules of the air.
— CAA restrictions on when and where you can fly.
— How an aerofoil works.
— The stall.
— Airspeed groundspeed & windspeed.
— Identifying areas of lift and turbulence
— Dealing with problems in flight.
— Basic weather and forecasts.

Sample questions for a Student level exam.
1. A hang-glider is circling in a thermal, you wish to use the same thermal what rule applies?
A. You must circle in the same direction as him.
B. You have right of way as he is faster and more manoeuvrable than you.
C. The lower pilot has right of way.
D. You must both circle to the left to reduce the risk of collision.

2. You are flying downwind with an airspeed of 17mph, the wind is 18mph. What is your Groundspeed?
A. 35 mph.
B. 1 mph.
C. 18 mph.
D. 17 mph.

Club pilot level
All the topics for student pilot plus:
— Cloud types (inc ground level)
— Basic air law
— Principles of flight, Lift/drag etc
— Restrictions on other types of paragliding activity. E.g power/ towing/dual etc.
— Unstable situations, spins, stalls, tucks etc.

Sample questions for a Club pilot level exam
1. Define VMC when flying in uncontrolled airspace above 3,000ft AMSL:
A. 5 nautical miles visibility, 1,000ft clear of cloud vertically and horizontally.
B. Clear of cloud and in sight of the surface with visibility of at least 5km.
C. 1,000ft clear of cloud vertically, & 1,500m horizontally with visibility of at least 5km.
D. Clear of cloud and in sight of the surface with visibility of at least one nautical mile.

2. A deep or parachutal stall can be caused:
A. By braking too deeply.
B. When recovering from "B lining".
C. By pulling on both rear risers.
D. By any of the above.

Pilot level

All the topics for Club pilot plus:
— Reading an airchart (including abbreviations symbols, scales, magnetic variations etc).
— Temperature and pressure gradients and rates.
— Aerodynamics & performance of a paraglider.
— Instruments.

Sample questions for Pilot level exam

1. What meteorological conditions could give rise to an inversion?
A. A high pressure area with extensive cloud cover during the night to trap convective heat.
B. A prolonged period of high pressure when the air has become dirty with trapped dust and smoke particles.
C. Warm air at altitude being pushed over colder air at ground level by an occluded front.
D. An air mass being warmed as it is compressed by sinking in the centre of a high pressure area.

2. The following symbol taken from an airchart shows:

A. A disused airfield with gliding activity.
B. A civil airfield with parachuting and winch cable activity.
C. A civil airfield with microlight and paragliding activity.
D. A military airfield with winch cable and parachuting activity.

Advanced pilot level

The topics for the advanced pilot paper are beyond the scope of this book. Essentially dealing with cross-country navigation skills.

How a paraglider is designed and built

40

Before any reputable dealer will sell a new paraglider it will have passed an independent airworthiness test. This test is designed to ensure that the wing has no hidden vices, will react correctly to proper control inputs and is sufficiently strong. It is worth mentioning that a number of prototypes — even from quite well known manufacturers — have failed such a test. Buying any paraglider without certification is not only likely to invalidate any insurance cover you may hold (including BHPA 3rd party cover) it will also be next to impossible to resell and could be bad for your health.

There are two main bodies awarding airworthiness certificates. The German DHV (manufacturers association) which gives the Guteseigel, and the ACPUL (AFNOR) system which is recognised in the rest of Europe. Both standards are acceptable in the UK and world-wide, though you are far more likely to come across the ACPUL system, and, in fact, CEN (the European standards institute) will almost certainly accept the latest proposed ACPUL tests as a Pan-European standard. For this reason this section concentrates on that test system.

During the last few years the ACPUL certification has been based upon a strength test and a number of flying tests. The flight tests are filmed

Laser plotter/cutter. (Airwave)

149

and, depending upon the behaviour of the wing, award an A B or C grade for each manoeuvre. Whilst the tests are far from perfect as they only simulate what may happen to a wing in various attitudes and cannot take account of turbulent air, for example, they do offer a reasonable guide to the relative stability of the canopy.

A grades are awarded to those that show fast and spontaneous recovery , B grades on those manoeuvres where some input is required or the wing is a little slower than ideal in recovering spontaneously, and C grades in case where expert input is required to prevent the situation deteriorating. Obviously any wing with a C grade is suitable only for a pilot with the relevant instability training.

Since October 94 the tests are basically as outlined below. A manufacturer puts forward his product to be tested at one of the following levels:

STANDARD (STD): those that have a combination of handling and stability intended to make them suitable for use by student and recreational pilots.

PERFORMANCE (PERF): those that have a combination of handling performance and stability intended to make them suitable for use by regular weekend/club competition level pilots. Such pilots can be expected to have some skill at avoiding and recovering from departures from normal flight.

COMPETITION (COMP): those that have a combination of handling, performance and stability intended to make them suitable for experienced national competition level pilots. Such pilots can be expected to be highly skilled at avoiding and recovering from departures from normal flight.

DUAL: suitable for Tandem (2 man) flight.

Load Test

The paraglider must successfully pass a load test with a payload equating to 8 times the maximum placarded payload— ie a wing with a weight range of 80-100kg will need to be able to withstand a load of 800kg without showing any structural damage.

There is also a shock load test where the wing is suddenly loaded to G. These tests are performed by pulling the wing at high speed with an 8 ton truck which is fitted with load cells and monitoring equipment.

Flight Tests

Note "trimmers"are referred to in almost every test. These are devices that alter and fix the wings angle of attack. They can radically alter its behaviour in unstable situations and so I advise that you choose a wing without trimmers fitted , or you leave them set at neutral unless you fully understand their use and function.

1. Launch
5 launches to be made. 3 out of 5 to show no abnormal characteristics.

STD - if trimmer fitted then 5 with slowest setting and 5 with fastest.

PERF/COMP/DUAL - trimmers set as per users manual.

2. Landing
The pilot must be able to land on his or her feet without the use of extraordinary skill.

STANDARD/DUAL - trimmers set to slowest and to fastest

PERF/COMP - trimmers as per manual.

3. Speed range
(slowest maintainable speed to highest maintainable speed)

STD/PERF/COMP - range must be at least 10kph.

DUAL - range must be at least 12kph.

4. Effects of trimmers and secondary speed controls (accelerators)
ALL - 10secs at minimum settable speed with no adverse behaviour.

- 10 secs at maximum speed (trimmers AND accelerator at max) with no adverse behaviour.

5. Pitch stability
Slowed to stall point and controls released.

STD - trimmers full on and full off. The wing must not dive more than 45 degrees and if it tucks may not alter course and must recover spontaneously.

PERF - trimmers full off. The leading edge shall not dive below 90 degrees, if it tucks it should not alter course by more than 90 degrees and spontaneously recover to normal flight.

COMP/ DUAL - not tested

6. Recovery form deep stall (with primary controls)
With trimmer set to slowest speed the wing is slowed to stall point , then controls are slowly and smoothly released.

STD - with no input the wing must recover to normal flight within 4 secs and shall not dive to more than 45 degrees above the horizon. Must not alter course by more than 90 degrees

PERF - with no input the wing must recover normal flight within 4 secs. The leading edge must not dive below the horizon.

COMP - with no input the wing shall recover within 4 secs or, if it remains in deep stall, the pilot shall use the procedure given in the manual. In this case the wing must recover within a further 4 secs. In either case the leading edge must not dive below the horizon. The wing may tuck but shall not alter course by more than 90 degrees.

DUAL with trimmers on and off - the wing must recover within 4 secs and must not dive below the horizon. The wing shall not alter course by more than 90 degrees.

7. Recovery from B line or similar deep stall (slow release)

Trimmers on, B lined until near vertical flight is achieved. Slow and smooth release.

STD (also done with trimmers off) - with no input the wing must resume normal flight within 4 secs. The leading edge shall not dive to more than 45 degrees above the horizon. The wing shall not alter course by more than 90 degrees.

PERF - with no input the wing must recover to normal flight within 4 secs. If the wing remains in deep stall the pilot shall use the procedure given in the manual to exit the stall. In the latter case the wing shall recover within a further 4 secs with no tucks. In either case the leading edge shall not dive below the horizon.

DUAL - as PERF but also tested with trimmers off.

COMP - not tested.

8. Recovery from B line stall or similar (fast release)

Trimmers off. Fast smooth release.

STD (also with trimmers on.) - with no pilot input the wing must recover normal flight within 4 secs. The leading edge shall not dive more than 45 degrees above the horizon. The wing may tuck but may not alter course.

PERF/COMP - with no input the wing must recover within 4 secs and not dive below the horizon. If not recovered within 4 secs the pilot must act in accordance with the manual and normal flight must be achieved within a further 4 secs. The wing may tuck but may not alter course by more than 90 degrees.

DUAL - as for PERF and COMP but also with trimmers on.

9. Turning ability

Trimmers set to slowest. 360 degree turn one way then reverse direction and 360 the other way, in normal flight. (No spins)

STD (also with trimmers off) - manoeuvre completed within 18 secs.

PERF - manoeuvre completed within 20 secs.

COMP - manoeuvre completed within 23 secs.

DUAL (also with trimmers off) - manoeuvre completed within 23 secs.

10. Spin tendency

Trimmers set to slowest. From no control instantly apply full control on one side (weight shift may also be used.) when turned 90 degrees control is released. (Tested both left and right).

STD (also with trimmers off) - the wing must remain under full control throughout

PERF - the wing must remain under full control throughout.

COMP - the wing must not depart from pilotable flight.

DUAL (also with trimmers off) - the wing must not depart from pilotable flight.

11. Turn reversal

Trimmers at slowest and at fastest. Rhythmic turns to obtain at least 45 degrees of bank.

STD/DUAL - no tucks shall occur

PERF - tucks may occur but the wing shall spontaneously recover normal flight within 90 degrees.

COMP - tucks may occur but the wing must spontaneously recover to pilotable flight within 90 degrees.

12. Asymmetric tuck recovery (immediate release)

Trimmers on fast. Quick 55 per cent tuck. Immediate release, weight transfer to tucked side.

STD (also with trimmers at slow) - the wing shall spontaneously recover to pilotable flight within 4 secs and 180 degrees.

PERF - the wing shall spontaneously recover to pilotable flight within 4 secs and 360 degrees.

COMP - if spontaneous recovery has not occurred within 4 secs or 360 degrees (whichever is sooner) the pilot shall intervene as per the manual and the wing shall regain pilotable flight within 90 degrees or 4 secs

DUAL - as COMP but also tested with trimmers at slow.

13. Recovery from maintained asymmetric tuck

Trimmers set at fastest. Tuck of 55 per cent of wing. Weight to tucked side. held in for 720 degrees then released.

STD/DUAL (also with trimmers at slowest) - the wing shall spontaneously recover to pilotable flight within 360 degrees.

PERF - if spontaneous recovery has not occurred within 360 degrees or 4 secs, then it must be possible to regain pilotable flight using actions from manual within 90 degrees and 4 secs.

COMP - if spontaneous recovery has not occurred within 360 degrees or 4 secs then it must be possible to regain pilotable flight using recommended actions within 360 degrees and 4 secs.

14. Spin recovery

Trimmers at fastest. From minimum speed, one control off the other on enough to induce a spin. Hold for 360 degrees, release quickly.

STD (also with trimmers at slowest) - the wing shall spontaneously return to normal flight, it may continue to turn in the direction of the spin for up to 360 degrees.

PERF - the wing may continue to spin for a maximum of a further 360 degrees, before spontaneous recovery to pilotable flight which shall occur within a further 90 degrees.

COMP - not tested.

DUAL (also with trimmers at slowest) - the wing shall return to pilotable flight in less than 720 degrees in the same direction.

15. Asymmetric stall recovery

Trimmers at fastest. Slowed to minimum speed. One control depressed further to induce asymmetric stall. Immediate release of both controls.

STD (also with trimmers on slowest) - the wing shall spontaneously recover normal flight without changing course more than 90 degrees.

PERF - if spontaneous recovery has not occurred within 180 degrees, the pilot shall intervene as per the manual and the wing shall regain normal flight within a further 90 degrees.

COMP - not tested.

DUAL (also with trimmers on slowest) - as PERF.

16. Symmetric tuck recovery

Trimmers set at fastest. A full front tuck and immediate release.

STD (also with trimmers on slowest) - with no input the wing shall recover pilotable flight within 4 secs without changing course. The leading edge shall not dive more than 45 degrees above the horizon.

PERF - if spontaneous recovery has not occurred within 4 secs the pilot shall intervene as per the users manual. The wing shall regain pilotable flight within a further 4 secs and without changing course by more than 90 degrees. The leading edge shall not dive below the horizon.

COMP/DUAL - not tested.

17. Spiral dive recovery

Trimmers at slowest. A tight spiral is induced and held for 720 degrees, the pilot slowly and smoothly allows the controls to return to the released position.

STD - the wing shall spontaneously recover and shall remain in the turn for less than 360 degrees.

PERF - the wing shall return to pilotable flight and shall show no tendency to tighten the turn.

COMP - if the wing has not recovered to pilotable flight within 360 degrees, the pilot may intervene as per the manual and the wing shall regain pilotable flight within 360 degrees.

DUAL - the wing shall spontaneously recover to normal straight flight within 720 degrees.

There is a terrific amount of information available in these tests . But even knowing all this is only part of the story — some wings, for example, have a tendency to enter a spin more easily than others and this is not measured in the tests. Also, the tests themselves, while thorough, are conducted in smooth air by very experienced pilots and this is no guarantee that the wing will behave in the same way in turbulence.

Finally, the test pilots are always flying at the correct weight for the canopy. IF YOU FLY OVER OR UNDER WEIGHT THEN STABILITY IN SOME SITUATIONS CAN BE SEVERELY COMPROMISED. Make sure you are the right weight for your wing.

If this is all a bit much to take in, as is probably the case if you are looking for your first paraglider, here is a shortened guide :

— If you are a new pilot and/or are not particularly interested in competitions — buy a wing with Standard certification.

— If you have a a few hours under your belt are an ambitious XC pilot and you have had some training in dealing with tucks etc, then the wings that have performance rating may be suitable for you.

— If you are an experienced pilot and have SIV experience and are interested in top-level competition, then the COMP level wings are likely to give you the edge you need.

— Best of all get advice.

AERO - TESTS	categorie/category	STANDARD
	No de conformite aux normes Reference numbe standards S52308 / S52309	95121623 AP
	date d'enregistrement date certified	7 / 12 / 95

CONSTRUCTEUR MANUFACTURER	APCO AVIATION
MODELE MODEL	SENTRA 28

Configuration lors des tests / Configuration during the tests

Poids total volant mini / Minimum flying weight	70	KG	Type de harnais / Type of harness	ABS
Poids total volant maxi / Maximum flying weight	90	KG	Constructeur / Manufacturer	APCO AVIATION
Poids du modèle / Weight of the model	7,5	KG	Modele / Model	TOP HARNESS
No. d'élévateur / No of risers	4		Réglage de la ventrale / Chest strap adjust	44
			Hauteur assise / maillon / Seat / maillons distance	40

Accessoires / Accessories

Débattement de l'accélérateur / Range of speed bar	17	cm
Débattement des afficheurs / Range of trimmers		cm
Plage de vitesse aux commandes / Brakes speed range	12	km/h
Plage de vitesse avec accessoires / Range with accessories	20	km/h
Révision / Check every	100 Heures / annuelle 100 flying hours / Yearly	
Attention: avant utilisation lire le manuel de vol Warning: before use refer to the user's manual		

Tests de conformite realises par / Conformity tests carried out by
AERO - TESTS
6 chemin de camperousse 06130 GRASSE FRANCE

Facsimile of an ACPUL test certificate

A brief guide to the world's manufacturers

41

Paragliders

ADG (Atelier de la Glisse): ADG SA- Z.A, 15 Rue des Aulnes, 67720 Hoerdt, France
☎ 88513044   Fax 88513043
Colbri 2/Alouette/Kiwi/Amazone/BI-Surf

Advance Advance Thun SA Seestrasse14 3602 Thun Switzerland
☎ 033 231118   Fax 033 231150
Epsilon/Sigma 3/Omega 3 /Bi-advance
Designer/owner: Robert Graham
Notes : (Hans Bollinger world champ '94 on Omega 3 proto)

Aerostudi Aerostudi SpA ,Via Colombara di Vigano 7, 34015 Muggia (TS), Italy
☎ 040 232252 Fax 040 232291
Marilyn
Notes : Little known Outside Italy

Airbow Airbow, Roggenweg 2, 13930 Sexten, Italy
☎ 0474 70104 Fax 0474 70030
Vulture Gryphus/Urubuh/Joy
Designer Roman Tschurtschenthaler

Ailes de K   Ailes De K SA , Riond Bosson 3 -1110 Morges, Switzerland
☎ 021 8023732 Fax 021 8023733
Genair/Flyair/Spydair/Cruisair/Sideair

Airwave   Airwave Gliders, Elm Lane, Shalfleet, Isle of Wight, PO30 4JY, England
☎ 01983 531611 Fax 0198378552
Reggae/Samba/Alto/AltoExtreme/Duet
Designers B Goldsmith and B Barnes

Atmos Spoflu Ag, Gartenstrasse 36, PO Box 8039, Zurich, Switzerland
☎ 01 2023316 Fax 01 2023305
Atmos

 Apco Aviation   Apco Aviation Ltd ,PO Box 2124 58121 ,Holon, Israel
☎ 972 9 334322 Fax 972 9 619051
Prima/Sabra/Spectra/Sentra/Xtra/Zen
Notes : Supra & Xtra world record holders @ 6/95 (Open distance & goal) 3yr fabric warranty since Jan 94

Blue Phoenix   Blue Phoenix Paragliding,Via Umberto Nobile, 14 36071 Arzignano (V1)

☎ and Fax 0444 676830/0336 468110/0337 518421
Light/Ace/ExtremeBIP

Condor man Condor Man Paragliders, 6710 Nenzing, Austria
☎ 5522 45488 Fax 5522 43856
Classic /Caesar/TornadoAlpamayo/Obelix

Custom Sail Custom Sail, Route de Broves, 83830Bargemon, France
☎ 94478212 Fax 94766074
HP/XPKL/XS

Delta Fly Delta Fly, Forchenweg 37, 71134 Aidlingen, Germany
☎ 07034 62609 Fax 07034 62666
Finesse

Easy Fly Easy Fly, Repubblica Ceca
Sprint/Easy Sprint

Edel Edel, Dae Kyo, PO Box 10049, Seoul, Korea
Orion/Space/Superspace2/Energy

FalhAwk Falhawk Co Ltd 3.5.4.,-203 Minamiohtsuka, Toshima-Ku - Tokyo 170, Japan
Acto Ar/Acto Super

Firebird Firebird, Htzleriderstrasse 15, 8959 Seeg Allgau, Germany
☎ 83641078 Fax 83641078
Dolphin/Marlin/G-Sport/Genesis

Flight Design Flight Design International, Sielminger strasse 65 -70771, Leinfelden-Echterdingen, Germany
☎ 711 795095 Fax 711 795090
A4/ A5 sport/ B3

Freestyle Paragliders Freestyle Paragliders, Via Segantini, 95 -38062 Arco (TN)
☎ 0337 459926 Fax 0464 532566
Lynx/Acro/Syncro/Twin/Tornado/Experience

Free X Airsports GMBH Nordliche Seestrasse 7, Ammerland, Germany. Fax 08177/8916
Frantic/Fiber

Fun 2 Fly Fun To Fly, South Africa
Profile/Reflex

Gypaaile 27 Rue St Anne, 65200 Gerde, France
☎ 62910460 Fax 62951454
Carlit/Arbizon/Palas/Swan

Harley Para dynamics Unit 40 Central Way, Cheltenham Trade Park, Cheltenham Glos. GL51 8LZ UK
☎ 01242 228869 Fax 01242 228807
Eclipse/Aurora

ITV ZAE les Glaisins 10, Rue du pre Felin, 74940 Annecy le vieux, France
☎ 50640183 Fax 50278606

Topaze/Agena/Nunki/Atkis/ Merak

Mac Paratechnology Po Box 26 CZ756-61 Roznov p.r. Czech Republic
Bobby/Nirvana/Vision

North Sails Seehauptstrasse 60 8122 Penburg, Germany
☎ 08856 9150   Fax 08856 1601
Sting/Dimension/Swan

Nova Bernhard Hoftel; Srasse 14 6020 Innsbruck Austria
☎ 512 361340   Fax 512 361342
Philou/Phocus/Zyon/Xenon

Paradelta Via Quasimodo, 3-43100 Parma Italy
☎ 0521 994630   Fax 0521 291573
Breeze/Basic/Blazer

Paratech Beim Aplenblick 9057 Weissbad Switzerland
P22/P40/P50/P5

Perche Probstener Strasse 15, 87637, Eisenberg, Germany
☎ 08364 8653   Fax 08364 8788
Graffity/Bliss/Aerologic/Dynamic

Pro design Larchenweg 33 6161 Natters, Austria
☎ 0512 546444   Fax 0512 546445
Challenger/Compact/Contest/Profeel

Stratos Stratos , Republica of Czechoslovakia
Proton/Exel

Swing Holdern 801 9038 Rehetobel, Austria
☎ 71952510   Fax 71951311
Picco/Prisma/Axis/Minoa/Mythos

Trekking BP 41 13410 Lambesc, France
☎ 42570590   Fax 42927754
Ritmo/Legend/Prelude/Oddessy

TechnicíAir 29 rue Madeleine, 23200 Aubusson, France
☎ 55838888   Fax 55838860
Koalas/Koyotts/Kolts/Skott

UP 113 Toranomon Minato-Ku-Tokyo 105 Japan
☎ 03 35932120   Fax 03 35042706
Boogie/Vision/Kendo/Pick Up

VTS V.T.S. Voileries Techniques Stephanoises, 4 rue E. Noirot 42100 St. Etienne
☎ 77418222   Fax 77419646
Birdy/Spoutnik/Liberty/Pacific

Harnesses

Apco Aviation ltd (qv)

Airwave ltd (qv)

Air Bulle Chemin des sources, 2ZI 38190 Crolles, France
☎ 76081521 Fax 760 88376

Alp Design S Masserini Via Roma 4 24020 Fiorano al Serio (BG)
☎ 035 714164 Fax 035 710493

Atmos (qv)
Charly Osterosch 3 8959 Seeg/Hitzleried Germany
☎ 08364 1286 Fax 08364 8426

Custom sail (qv)

Dimensione Volo :Via Caose 9 31030 Borso del Grappa TV Italy ****
☎ 0423 542087 Fax 0423 54030

Freestyle (qv)

Firebird(qv)

Metamorphosi 12034 Paesana CN Italy ****
☎ 0175 945392 Fax 0175 987070

Perche(qv)

Pro design (qv)

Skyline : W. Genghammer Stegenhauser 7, 83236 Ubersee/Chiemsee,
Germany
☎ 08642 267 Fax 08642 765

Sky Systems Edburton, Henfield, BN5 9LL UK.
☎ 01273 857700 Fax 01273 857722

Supáir 12 Avenue de Mandalaz, 74000 Annecy France
☎ 50457529 Fax 50527870

UP (qv)

Vonblon 8081 Lansberied Germany
☎ 08141 21730 Fax 08141 16939

Woody Valley Via al Catellere 38100 Trento Italy
☎ 0461931119 Fax 0461 935738

Reserves

APCO Aviation Ltd (qv) *MAYDAY (4 sizes 24m-42)*
Airwave (qv)   *ASS (24m/30m)*
Charly (qv)   *GS1 (2 sizes 31m & 35m)*
Custom sail (qv)   *CUSTAIR (2 sizes-33m& 38m)*
Edel (qv)   *SECURAMAX*

Firebird (qv)   *RS2 (34m)*
Junkers Profil   *PLUS (6 sizes 23m-48m)*
Metamorphosi (qv)   *P (4 sizes 18-42m)*
Paradelta (qv)   *PD (5 sizes 23m-45m)*
Perche (qv)   *OSCAR/ COLUMBUS (6 sizes 31m-85m)*
Pro design (qv)   *HELP (3 sizes 30m-36m)*
Sigma   *MINITEX (3sizes 29-50m)*
Skyline (qv)   *SURVIVAL (34m)*
Sup air (qv)   *SUP AIR (35m)*
Trekking (qv)   *F series (7sizes 31m-57m)*
UP (qv)   *LARA (3 sizes)*

Flying instruments

Afro   Bahnhofstrasse 37, 83253 Rimsting, Germany
☎ 08051 61249   Fax 08051 62036

Aircotec   Ebenaustrasse 10, Postfach 56, 6048 Horw, Switzerland
☎ 041 485887   Fax 041 487078

Brauniger Putrichstrasse 21, 8120 Weilheim, Germany
☎ 0881 64750   Fax 0881 4561

Davron   1 Church Rd, Keston, Kent, UK
☎ 01689 856723   Fax 01689 851823

Digifly   Via Perderanza 13, 40050 Villanova , Bologna, Italy
☎ 051 780658   Fax 051 781328

Flytec   Ebenaustrasse 8A, 6048 Horw, Switzerland
☎ 041 473424   Fax 041 485424

Fairhaven   47 Dales rd Spondon Derby UK DE21 7DG
☎ 01332 670707

Mastair   Elmatek, Rue des sources, 38920 Crolles, France
☎ 76080460   Fax 760893661

Pretel   ZI Les Bauches BP 25, 38640 Claix, France
☎ 76981026   Fax 76985778

Skybox ATW, Erlenbrunnenstrasse 20, 72411 Bodelhausen, Germany
☎ 07471 72033   Fax 07471 71747

Skywatch   JDC Electronics SA, Rue des Uttins 40, 1400 Yverdon les Bains, Switzerland
☎ 024 242121   Fax 024 242123

Thommen   4437 Waldenburg, Switzerland
☎ 061 9652222   Fax 061 9618171

Wasmer   Larkenweg 10, 79183 Waldkirch, Germany
☎ 07681 8187   Fax 076814434

Ian Currer

Take off at Gilboa launch Israel

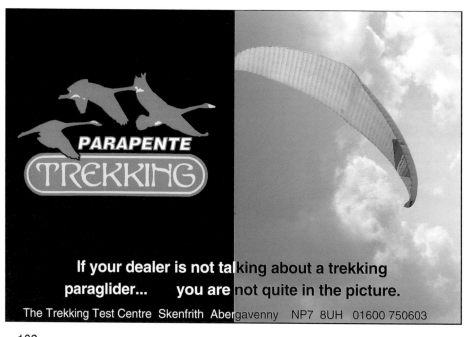

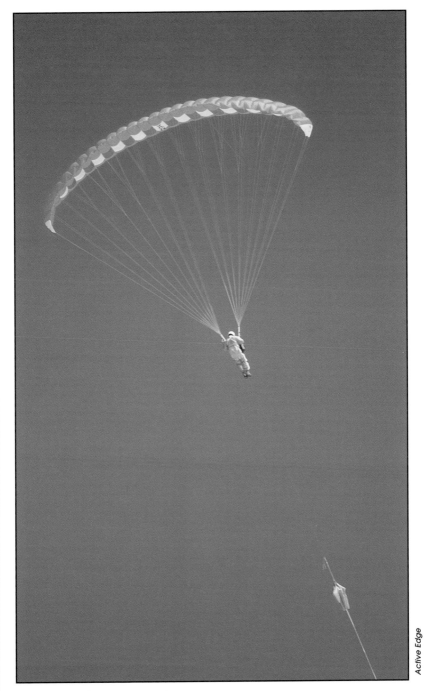

Nova Phoenix on tow launch

Glossary of terms

"A" line — Line to the leading edge of the wing

ACPULS — European airworthiness testing body

Aerodynamics — The study of moving air

Aerofoil — The shape of a section through a wing

Airspeed — The speed of the aircraft through the air

Angle of attack — The angle at which the airflow meets the wing

Aspect ratio — The ratio of the span to the average chord (width) of the wing

ATZ — Aerodrome traffic zone

Batten — Stiffener in the wing (usually plastic or glass fibre)

Brake — Control to alter the speed or direction of the paraglider

"B" line stall — A manoeuvre to disrupt the smooth flow over a wing by pulling down the "B" lines

Chord — Distance from the leading edge to the trailing edge at any given point

Cirrus — Very high ice clouds

Cumulus — A "heaped" cloud found above thermals

Drag ailerons — The correct term for the control system on a paraglider

Dyneema — A type of line material

Flare — Either, the action of applying full brake hard to slow down on landing; or a triangular piece of cloth that helps to distribute evenly the load from a line

Glide ratio — Ratio of distance travelled horizontally to the height lost

GPS (Global positioning system) — A hand held navigational instrument.

Groundspeed — The speed of the aircraft over the ground

Keeper — A ring sewn to the rear riser to retain the control line

Kevlar — A type of line material

Lift — Either, the upward force created by the action of the aerofoil; or, air that is rising faster than the wing is sinking

Lapse rate — The rate of temperature decrease with height

Maillon Rapide — Trade name of the steel links used to connect the lines to the risers and, sometimes, risers to harness

MATZ — Military aerodrome traffic zone

Min(imum) sink rate — The canopy's slowest rate of descent

Pitch — Rotation of an aircraft through lateral axis (nose up or down)

PLF — Parachute landing fall

Polyester — Type of canopy fabric

Rip-stop nylon — Type of canopy fabric

Riser — Webbing connecting the harness to lines

Roll — Rotation of an aircraft through its longitudinal axis (banking)

Sink — Descending air

Stall — Point at which the airflow over the wing breaks away and there is no longer sufficient lift to support the aircraft

Thermal — Bubble or column of rising air

Wind gradient — Reduction in windspeed near the ground, due to friction

Conversions

1 knot	=	1.15 mph
1 mph	=	1.609 kph
1 kph	=	0.622 mph
1 kg	=	2.204 lbs
1,000ft	=	305 metres
1000m	=	3,280 ft

• APPENDICES •

Further reading

ⓘ

Airlaw
Cap 85, *CAA Publication*
BHGA Pilot Handbook
Microlight Pilot's Handbook, *Brian Cosgrove*
Understanding Gliding, *D Piggott*
Walking on Air, *Dennis Pagen*
An Introduction to Paragliding, *Z Frankel*

Meteorology
Flying Conditions, *Dennis Pagen*
Understanding Weather, *T Bradbury*
Understanding the Sky, *Dennis Pagen*

Useful addresses

ⓘⓘ

British Hang Gliding & Paragliding Association
The Old School Room, Loughborough Road
Leicester
LE1 5PJ

American Paragliding Association
25 Goller Place
Staten Island, NY 10314,
USA

French Paragliding Association
3 rue Ampère
94200 Ivry-sur-Seine,
France

How it all started: Jan Nielson foot launches a 9 cell free-fall jump chute.

freeX airsports - uk distribution lyon equipment.
dent, sedbergh, cumbria, la10 5ql   tel 015396 25493 - fax 015396 25454

fully equipped specialist repair service to all makes of paraglider

Index

Above: Hi-Lite soaring over Lake Annecy. (K. Moore)

Top: Busy day at Chillerton on the Isle of Wight. (S. Fenwick)

Above: *Worm's eye view of Michel Carnet of Sky Systems. (Sky Systems)*

Top: *Ski launch in the Alps. (L. Moore)*

171

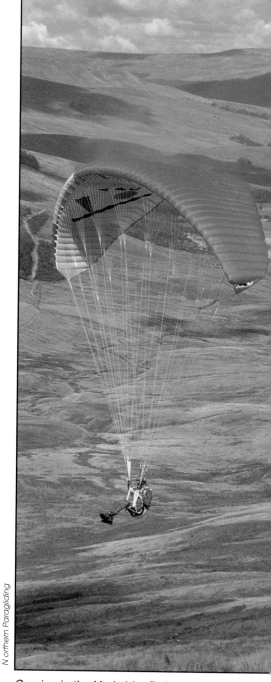

N orthern Paragliding

Soaring in the Yorkshire Dales

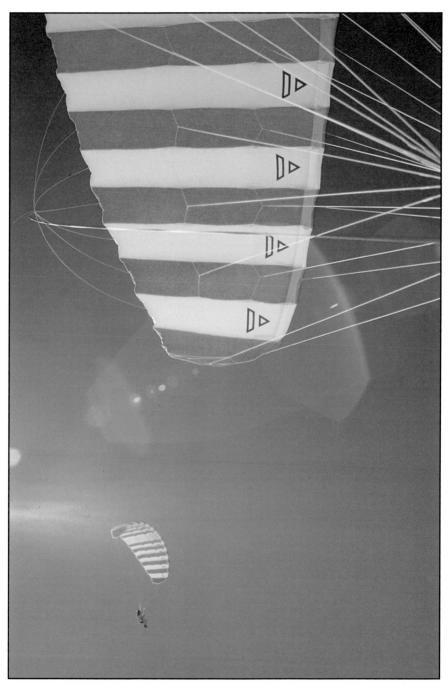

Fun-Air Chirons wing to wing. (Pink Sport)

TOUCHING *Cloudbase*

THE VIDEO: Although the book contains a great deal of information it cannot show you how an air foil actually works in a wind tunnel, do a pre-flight check, or demonstrate how to master a cross-brake launch.

No static illustration can show how to recover from a collapse or illustrate what a spin looks like. And of course a book can never get over the sheer grace and exhilaration of flying these incredible machines... So we made a video!

The tape is 1 hr long and covers all these things, as well as many of the other subjects covered in the book. It comes with a handy index to allow you to fast forward refer to any particular point, and it is available in PAL (European) or NTSC (USA & Japan) format.

THE CD ROM: When publishing the book we had scores of excellent photos and diagrams to choose from but were constrained to just a few by the printing process. As any student knows spoken words are easier than written words to take in, and certain topics can only be done justice by the moving image.

The CD format removes these barriers. Our software package contains many times the number of images we could fit into the book and has allowed us, where appropriate, to include video sequences.

The easy-to-follow "click on a picture" format makes it child's play to select the subject you want, and explore the world of paragliding in an interactive medium... Some day all books will be this way...(next step virtual paragliding?) The CD Rom will be available from Autumn '96 from Touching Cloudbase outlets, or by mail from the address below:

Air Supplies: Dunvegan Lodge, Front Street, Barmby Moor, York. YO4 5EB.
Tel: 01759 304404   Fax: 01759 306747.

The video costs £25.00 inc p&p.
The CD Rom is expected to cost around £35.00.

PARAMOTORING

The ultimate portable aircraft! Your motor and wing will fit into the back of an average family car. The paramotor is a partnership between a paraglider, a small two stroke engine and a propeller offering the lightest of powered aircraft. The motors weigh in at 15kg and range in capacity from 80cc to 200cc.

Northern Paramotoring are now offering training courses near York in this amazing new sport

Send for an information pack now!

☎ 01904 470068

Power to the people!

Above the Lake District

Lakes Paragliding

Fun-Air Chiron and Bull Ball approaching landing in the Swiss Alps. (Pink Sport)

NORTHERN
PARAGLIDING CENTRE
Information pack from:

Ian Currer   ☎ 01759 304404
Rob & Neil Cruickshank ☎ 01931 715100

or write to:

Dunvegan Lodge
Front Street
Barmby Moor
York YO4 5EB

> **For courses in
> the Yorkshire Dales**

Who are Northern Paragliding? The school started life in 1988 when **Ian Currer**, who up to that point had been involved in hang-gliding, saw the potential of the new sport of paragliding. He was joined in 1989 by **Rob Cruickshank** and the school has grown rapidly to become one of the largest in the UK. Ian and Rob saw the need for a publication to introduce the sport to students and explain the theoretical side of the sport. **'Touching Cloudbase'** was first published in 1991. **Neil Cruickshank**, Rob's brother *(competition pilot and instructor)* joined the team in 1995. We are committed to providing first class training to all levels in paragliding and more recently paramotoring.

Where are we? We are based in the beautiful **Yorkshire Dales** and work from a converted chapel in the village of Burtersett within sight of some of the most spectacular sites in the country *(Wether Fell, Semer Water, Stags Fell)*. Our sites are quiet, uncrowded and cover all wind directions. The centre has a purpose built shop and lecture facilities and low cost accommodation is available within minutes of our door.

Who will teach you to fly? We have a team of instructors from a variety of backgrounds, from teachers to ski instructors. They are all active pilots with many years of experience and are keen to impart their knowledge to our students. We never forget however, that we are all doing this for fun, a good time, as well as good flying, is guaranteed!

Paramotoring? We are already teaching in the south of France and will have a UK base set up in the UK by the time you read this. Try the ultimate portable aircraft - fits in the back of a Golf hatchback with the seats down!! Call Rob or Neil for an information pack.

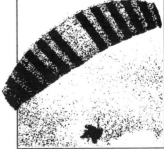

XC

thermals

ParAvion

tuition . theory lectures . spares . repairs . gift vouchers . equipment : UP . edel . apco . airwave . flight design . solar wings . sup'air .airbulle . skyline .

cloud streets

second chanz . mayday . metamorfosi . vertiflex . brauniger . davron . aircotec . digifly . flytec . avocet . garmin . skywatch . windwizard . dwyer . casio . silva . charly . alinco . airtalker .

base

salomon . crispi . scarpa . fly . pick up . icaro . uvex . romer . camelbak . glider rider . system x . animal . bei . o-zee . calange . stubai . maillon rapide .

kilometres

open 7 days a week: ParAvion

Elm Tree Park Manton Marlborough
Wiltshire SN8 1PS Tel: 01672 861380
Fax: 01672 861580

185

Airwave Black Magic in the French Alps. (Airwave)

Index of Advertisers

Acknowledgements

Rob & I would like to thank the following people who have contributed a great deal of help and expertise, and given valuable feedback on the first edition of this book.

Bernard Kane MBE, Former Chairman of the BHPA Safety & Training Committee

Andy Cowley, Current Chairman of Safety & Training

Walter Neumark

Les Smallwood (STC Member and Air-traffic controller)

Fred Stockwell. Editor of *Paragliding* Magazine (USA)

Airwave Gliders Ltd

Apco Aviation Ltd

Eddie Close

Jolyon Harrison

And the rest of the team — Shaun, Paul, Jackie, Sandrine, Sue and Neil.

Northern Paragliding

The author about to launch tandem in a good wind — with a little help from some friends.

Active Edge

Nova Phocus launching in the snow

Fred Stockwell

RAF rescue helicopter recovers an injured pilot — Don't let it be you!

This air-to-air shot clearly shows the diagonal rib technology now being incorporated into some new wings. (Glider — Apco Sentra)